LEADING LADIES

LEADING LADIES

HISTORICAL PROFILES

OF WOMEN

IN LEADERSHIP

CAPT. ALAN HODGES

TATE PUBLISHING
AND ENTERPRISES, LLC

Published by Tate Publishing & Enterprises, LLC
127 E. Trade Center Terrace | Mustang, Oklahoma 73064 USA
1.888.361.9473 | www.tatepublishing.com

Tate Publishing is committed to excellence in the publishing industry. The company reflects the philosophy established by the founders, based on Psalm 68:11,
"The Lord gave the word and great was the company of those who published it."

Book design copyright © 2011 by Tate Publishing, LLC. All rights reserved.
Cover design by Kenna Davis
Interior design by Chelsea Womble

Published in the United States of America

ISBN: 978-1-61346-244-7
1. Biography & Autobiography, Women
2. History, General
11.09.07

ACKNOWLEDGMENTS

I wish to record my thanks to Dan Manor of the Ministry of Tourism, Government of Israel for his invaluable assistance with the biblical women of this book;

To forensic anthropologist Stevie Spurlin, for her suggestion to include a chapter on Esther, one of the better chapters;

To my daughters, JoAnne and Louise, for their unflagging support in this venture;

To Dr. Condoleezza Rice, from whom I got the inspiration to write this book.

TABLE OF CONTENTS

PREFACE

More things are wrought by prayer

Than this world dreams of, Wherefore, let thy voice

Rise like a fountain …

> Lord Alfred Tennyson, *Morte D'Arthur*

Nothing in life is to be feared. It is only to be understood.

> Marie Curie

I fear nothing but treachery.

> Joan of Arc

Leading Ladies: Historical Profiles of Women in Leadership is a tribute to women. It is about you and is written to inspire you to "rise up," improve yourself and your self-esteem, and to do great things.

All the women in this book have two things in common; courage and sheer determination. Read the stories and learn how each of these heroines accomplished their goals and achieved their places in history. Invite the spirits of these great women to come into your soul as you read about them and their deeds. You will emerge all the better for it.

As for your aims and ambitions, they can be achieved if you focus your thought forces on them.

Take note of Condoleezza Rice's quote before the story of Deborra. You could be that "one person."

I use the term "thoughts forces," but you might call it prayer as most of the ladies in this book did or do. Your thoughts and prayers will only be effective and answered if they are transmitted with pure, unconditional love. Focus your thought forces on where you would like to be. Banish negative thoughts, and radiate love as you walk through life, to all. That alone is going to make you feel good about yourself and make others around you have a brighter day.

You are going to encounter racism, sexism, and social injustice in almost all of these stories, and you will learn how these magnificent women overcame all their obstacles, each in her own way.

Shoot for the stars!

DEBORRA:
THE MOTHER OF ISRAEL

Anytime you feel powerless to affect your world, remember all you have learned about the history of our world. That history teaches that it takes just a single, determined individual to bring profound change …

Condoleezza Rice

Deborra's story takes place in the twelfth century before Christ and is an account of one woman's leadership of her country in troubled times. Deborra is regarded by many as the Jewish Joan of Arc. There was a total lack of leadership in Israel at that time, a situation which she decided to rectify. This situation exists in our country today. Interestingly, we actually have two strong women probably going to run for the highest office in the land. Deborra's story could well apply to any woman aspiring to an elected office.

The book of Judges covers one of the darkest periods of Israel's long and turbulent history. Deborra was the fourth and only female judge of pre-monarchic Israel. The book tells us that a judge was the secular leader of the children of Israel and so "judged" Israel. Deborra was a sitting judge as we think of judges today, and tried legal cases and rendered judicial decisions.

She held court sitting under a palm tree, named for her, between Ramah in Benjamin and Bethel in the land of Ephraim. To have held court and tried men in her home would have been considered to be the height of impropriety.

She was also a prophetess and is one of the only five women mentioned in the Bible as prophets. She taught the Talmud to her audiences. Deborra's name means "bee."

She was married, and her husband was named Lappidoth, which means "torches." That name is not found anywhere in the Bible other than in the Book of Judges. Scholars feel that it may be assumed that the name really attests to Deborra's fiery spirit.

The Israelites were ever prone to stray from the paths of righteousness, ignoring God's commandments and practicing self-indulgence. God always punished His children very severely for their transgressions, sometimes enslaving them, sometimes having them conquered by foreign powers. When they repented and begged for forgiveness, a judge would rise among them and lead them out from their tribulation. Deborra concentrated her mental powers and "raised herself up" and became the fourth judge of Israel.

Israel had been under the heel of Jabin, the king of the Canaanites, for twenty years. Deborra decided that it was time to deliver her people once again. She appointed Barak, the king of Kadesh, to lead an army against the Canaanites. Barak's name means "lightning."

Deborra directed Barak to take ten thousand men from the Naphtali and Zebulun tribes, and lead them up to Mount Tabor where they would camp prior to their assault on the Canaanite army. Deborra said that she would bring the Canaanite army, under the command of General Sisera, to the River Kison, which flows through the Jezreel Valley, close to Mount Tabor. She referred to it as the "torrent of Kison," and as it was the rainy season, she knew that the river was in spate.

Barak said that unless Deborra accompanied him, he would not go. Deborra said, "I will surely go with thee notwithstanding that the journey thou takest shall not be for thine honor, for the Lord shall sell Sisera into the hand of a woman."

Mount Tabor has been of considerable strategic military importance since the earliest times. It overlooks the important road junction of the north-south Via Maris and the east-west highway of the Jezreel Valley. Countless battles have been fought there in both ancient and modern times; Deborra and Barak versus the Canaanites, Alexander of Judaea versus Gabinius, and the first Jewish-Roman War. During the Crusades, the mountain changed hands many times. Napoleon Bonaparte fought there against the Mamluks. In the 1948 Arab-Israeli War, the Golani Brigade fought the Arab Liberation army there.

Mount Tabor is also the probable site of the transfiguration of Christ (Luke 9:28–36). There is a church dedicated to that event on the top of the mountain.

The Canaanite army was very powerful and boasted nine hundred iron chariots. The opposing armies clashed on the riverbank, during a cloudburst, where Sisera's chariots quickly bogged down. Barak's infantry made short work of the charioteers and pursued the rest of the Canaanite army, which was now in full flight, and defeated it in detail. General Sisera fled on foot to the tent of Chaber, a Kenite tent maker, where he sought succor.

Chaber's wife, Jael, went out to greet Sisera and assured him that he would be safe.

Sisera asked Jael for a little water as his flight had made him thirsty. Jael opened a bottle of milk and gave it to him and bade him lay down to rest. She covered him up with a blanket. Sisera asked Jael to stand by the door and deny his presence, should anyone come looking for him.

As he slept, Jael took a tent peg and a mallet and drove the peg through Sisera's temple and into the ground.

Barak *was* looking for Sisera and Jael went out to meet him and announced that she would deliver Sisera to him. Thus was Deborra's prophecy fulfilled, and the children of Israel went on to enjoy forty years of peace.

Source: The Septuagint: Book of Judges.

JUDITH:
BEAUTY AND THE BEAST

There are those that say we have the custom to eat cheese on Chanukah to commemorate the miracle when Judith fed cheese to the enemy.

Rabbi Moshe Isseries

This is the story of a brave and beautiful woman who was prepared to risk her life and her honor, in the service of her country. While the menfolk vacillated and even considered surrendering to a cruel enemy, Judith made her own daring plan and executed it.

Around 650 years before Christ, King Nebuchadnezzar, who reigned over Assyria from his capital at Nineveh, decided to expand his empire by the usual method—military conquest. Some things never change.

The king of the Medes, one Arphaxad, had brought many smaller nations under his rule, and had built, even by biblical standards, an enormously strong citadel—Ectbatana. Unfortunately for him, all his horses and all his men could not prevail against the army of the Assyrians under the command of General Holofernes.

After this stellar victory, the Assyrian king began to suffer from the ultimate delusion of grandeur—that of having the whole known world bow to him as a god. To give the devil his due, he sent out ambassadors and tried diplomatic means to attain his goal. This effort proved to be disappointing as most of the kingdoms were quite rude to his emissaries and sent them packing.

This did not sit well with His Majesty, and he sent a huge army of one hundred and twenty thousand infantry, and twelve thousand cavalry (mounted archers) under the command of the trusty Holofernes to avenge these insults and to annihilate the non-conformists.

Holofernes was a past master of this form of warfare, popularly known as "scorched earth" policy.

Eventually he and his host arrived at the Plain of Damascus, during the harvest, and laid the land waste by fire and slaughter. The kings and princes of Syria, Mesopotamia, Syria Sobal, Libya, and Cilicia feared greatly for their countries and fiefdoms and accordingly sent their own emissaries with "garlands, and lights, and dances, and tumbrels, and flutes."

The ambassadors suggested that they would submit to the Assyrian king, pay homage, and become vassal states if Holofernes would leave them in peace. These diplomatic overtures were met with violence, and the general destroyed their cities and cut down their groves.

Upon receiving these tidings, the hearts and minds of the Israelites who lived in Judea were filled with horror and dread. They were particularly concerned with the safety of Jerusalem and the temple of their Lord. They walled their cities and prepared for war.

The high priest, Eliachim, wrote to all the people that lived on or near the mountain passes, urging them to take to the mountains and defend the roads that led to Jerusalem. He ordered all to pray to God and wear haircloths and ashes.

The town of Bathulia, now the city of Jenin, was in a very good defensive position as it overlooked both the Jordan and Jezreel valleys, and the passes were only wide enough for two horsemen to ride abreast.

When Holofernes learned that the Israelites were prepared to make a fight of it and had blockaded all the mountain passes, he flew into a rage and demanded to know what sort of people they were and who was their king.

The leader of the Ammonites, Achior, decided to visit Holofernes' camp under safe passage and tell him all about the Israelites' heritage, their beliefs, their legendary wanderings, their captivity in Egypt, and the destruction of the Egyptian army in the Red Sea. He also told Holofernes that if the Israelites stayed on the straight and narrow, their God had protected them and enabled them to overcome their enemies without swords or shields.

The last part was received with derision by the general and his captains, and they had a mind to kill Achior there and then but instead decided to have Achior lead some soldiers up into the mountains where they would slay some of the bravest Israelites and stab Achior a few times for good measure. Every nation must be shown that there is no god other than Nebuchadnezzar.

So Achior led a company of Assyrian soldiers up into the mountains where they were greeted by a party of Israelites armed with slings and stones. The Israelites drove off the Assyrians who left Achior tied to a tree.

Rescued by the townspeople, Achior related his experiences with Holofernes, who had sworn to come to Bathulia and slay all its inhabitants. Achior himself was to be tortured to death for suggesting that the children of Israel had a god more powerful than the king of Assyria.

The townsfolk fell to the ground, and there was much weeping, wailing, and gnashing of teeth, imploring God not to forsake them in their hour of peril. When prayers were complete, Achior was treated to a banquet, after which the night was spent in prayer.

On the next day Holofernes ordered the destruction of Bathulia and its entire population.

Finding the mountain passes too well defended by armed men, he sent scouting parties out round the town who quickly discovered fountains that fed an aqueduct into the town, which was immediately cut off. Upon further inspection they found springs outside the walls from which the townspeople were secretly drawing their water. The general ordered that a hundred men be posted to guard each of the springs, and he decided to lay siege to the town—another time tested military tactic.

The elders of Bathulia decided that if God did not come to their aid after five days and nights of prayer, they would attempt to parley with Holofernes and perhaps arrange a peaceful settlement. One of the prominent citizens of Bathulia was a woman named Judith who could not believe what she was hearing—that they would dare to give God a deadline.

Judith was a rich widow whose husband, Manasses, a wealthy farmer, had died of a heart attack supervising the harvesting of his barley crop three and a half years prior. Judith was an exceptionally beautiful woman. She lived alone with her maidservants and led a pious life.

She told the elders that she was not at all impressed with their strategy, which, in modern parlance, would be to "roll over and play dead." She had a much better plan in her mind, one which had proven to be successful since the beginning of time—seduction. She urged the elders not to enquire or attempt to uncover her plan but to pray for her and do nothing until she brought them word of the success of her mission. Ozias, the prince of Judea, gave Judith his blessing, and he the other elders left Judith alone to work on her design.

Judith went home and, wearing sackcloth and ashes, prostrated herself before God and prayed for strength to go forward with her plan.

When she felt strong enough, she shed her widow's weeds, washed and anointed herself with the best ointment, dressed her hair, and put on some her finest clothes and jewelry. The book of Judith tells us that God made her even more attractive because all of her preparation did not come from sensuality, but from virtue.

She gave her maid servant a bottle of wine, a vessel of oil, some parched corn, dry figs, and bread and cheese to carry, and they set out for the Assyrian camp. At the city gate, she found all the elders waiting, who did not try to stop her but wished her good luck and Godspeed.

Judith and her maid approached the camp. At around daybreak, they were approached by sentries who demanded to know whom she was and from whence she came and to where she was headed. Judith explained that she was a daughter of the Hebrews and that she knew that her people would never surrender nor seek terms. She said that she wanted to meet with General Holofernes and tell him of the Israelites' secrets and show him how he could overcome them without the loss of one man of his army.

The sentries were, of course, overcome by her beauty and, saying that she was doing the right thing, took her to the general's tent. Holofernes and his officers were immediately enraptured. The officers said, "Who can despise the people of the Hebrews who have such beautiful women, that we should not think it worth our while for their sakes to fight against them?"

Holofernes was sitting under a bejeweled canopy, and making sure that he had had a chance to take a good look at her, Judith prostrated herself at his feet.

The general at once asked her to be seated at his table, declaring that she had nothing to fear from him as he had never hurt a person that was willing to serve Nebuchadnezzar, the king. He went on to say that he would never have lifted a finger against her people had they not despised him. "So now let's get down to the reason that you have left your people and come to us," he said.

Judith then said some very flattering things about Nebuchadnezzar and Holofernes. She said that if the general would listen to her and do as she suggested, the god of the Hebrews would reward him handsomely.

She went on to tell him that the Israelites were behaving in a manner that was not tolerated by their god, that they were eating and drinking consecrated things, planning to kill their cattle and drink their blood. A famine was already upon them, and it is certain that their god would give them up for destruction. She said that the Lord had sent her to tell him of these things.

Judith then asked to go outside and pray to God, who would tell her when he would repay the Israelites for their manifold sins. She said that God would tell her how to bring the Assyrians into the center of Jerusalem, where the people would be like sheep without a shepherd and not so much as a dog would bark against them.

God was angry with the Israelites and had commanded that she should tell Holofernes these things.

The general and his staff were completely taken in by Judith, who they felt was unequalled in beauty and knowledge. Holofernes vowed that if all these things came to pass, he would accept her god as his, and she would be great in the house of Nebuchadnezzar and renowned throughout the earth.

Holofernes then invited her to eat from his table, but Judith said that she had to be careful not to slip into sinful ways but would eat the provisions that she had brought with her. Holofernes also gave Judith her own tent. She requested that that she be allowed to go out at night and pray to her god. The general issued orders that she be allowed to come and go as she pleased for three days.

During her nighttime excursions, she went into the valley of Bathulia, bathed, and prayed hard.

On the fourth day, Holofernes ordered his eunuch, Vagao, to "persuade that Hebrew woman" to join him for an evening of eating and drinking and merriment and to be honored by him. It was offensive to Holofernes's machismo that this beautiful woman had not succumbed to his charms, and it was considered shameful by Assyrian manhood standards that this state of affairs existed between Judith and him. Vagao hastened to assure her that she would not be in any danger. As the general was unwittingly playing right into her hand, she demurely accepted the invitation, saying that she would do her best to please the great man for the rest of her life.

Judith dressed carefully and went into Holofernes's tent. For his part he was totally smitten and burning with lust for her and suggested that she sit down and enjoy the evening.

Judith said, "I will drink, my lord. Because my life is magnified this day above all of my days." She ate and drank the food and wine that her maid had prepared for her.

Not so Holofernes, who was so excited that he drank more wine than he had ever drunk before in his life. It was growing late. Vagao and the servants withdrew as they had overindulged a bit too.

Judith was alone with Holofernes in his tent.

General Holofernes had passed out on his bed. Judith ordered her maid to stand outside and keep a lookout. Judith had one more communion with God and, praying for strength, drew Holofernes's saber, grabbed a handful of his hair, and, with two strokes, beheaded him. She took down the canopy over the bed and rolled his headless body up in it. Next she told her maid to put the severed head into the bag in which they normally carried their provisions.

The two women went out into the night as usual and walked to the walls of Bathulia and called out to the watchmen who, upon recognizing her voice, summoned all the townspeople to the gate. Judith commanded silence and revealed the head of the late General Holofernes, saying that God had answered their prayers by slaying the enemy of their people by the hand of a woman.

She then ordered the head to be hung on the city's walls at daybreak and that at sunrise, the entire town take up arms and proceed in battle formation toward the Assyrian camp.

Achior was so overcome that he prostrated himself before Judith and submitted himself to circumcision, declaring his undying faith to the Hebrew god.

At dawn the Israelites left Bathulia and advanced toward the Assyrian encampment. The Assyrian sentries upon seeing the armed host approaching, ran to their captains who in turn went to their leader's tent to awake him by their clamor and to get ready for battle.

"The mice are coming out of their holes and have presumed to challenge us to fight," they cried. But no response was forthcoming from Holofernes, so Vagao entered the tent and assuming that the general was sleeping with Judith, clapped his hands, but still no response. Vagao tore of the canopy round Holofernes's body and discovered his headless torso lying in its own blood. Weeping and rending his garments, he rushed to Judith's tent and found that it too was empty. Vagao confronted the Assyrian captains, screaming that one woman had done such an unimaginable thing to the house of Nebuchadnezzar.

Learning of the dreadful fate of their leader, the army panicked and fled from the Israelites in disorder. The latter were in close pursuit and slaughtered as many Assyrians as they could find. The older citizens who did not participate in the chase methodically stripped the Assyrian camp of booty and domestic animals, which took them over thirty days.

The high priest, Joachim, came from Jerusalem with an entourage of elders to pay homage to the hero-ine. There was feasting, music, and dancing, lasting for three months.

Judith lived to be one hundred and five and, upon her death, freed her faithful handmaiden. She was buried alongside her husband.

Source: Septuagint: Book of Judith

ESTHER: JEWISH QUEEN OF PERSIA

And the king loved Esther, and she found favour beyond all the other virgins; and put on her the queen's crown.

Esther 2:17

Esther's story is from the Book of Esther, and is of a beautiful young woman who saved her people from extermination. There was an element of luck involved, as there is in many of these stories. In Esther's case it was being in the right place at the right time. The rest is Esther.

In the third year of his reign, Xerxes I (Ahasueraus), king of Persia, whose dominions extended from India to Ethiopia, gave a great feast for his court, the nobles and princes of his provinces, and the armies of Persia and Media. The feast lasted for six months, and when it was over, the king gave another feast for the people of the capital, Shushan.

Xerxes's queen, Vashti, whose name means "beautiful," gave a banquet for the women of the royal household. On the seventh day of the king's banquet for the people, Xerxes became a little under the weather. It was hardly surprising since he had been partying for over six months. He instructed some of his chamberlains to go to Vashti and order her to the king's presence in order that her beauty might be seen by all. The queen declined the invitation.

This refusal, bordering on insolence, could not be tolerated, as it was not only insulting to the king, but if left unpunished would set a dangerous precedent; for if the queen could disobey the king, why shouldn't other wives disobey *their* husbands?

After consultation with his top advisors, Xerxes decided that Vashti would have to be replaced as queen. He therefore ordered that all the beautiful virgins in his kingdom be brought to the harem in Shushan and be placed in the care of Hegai, the eunuch who was the keeper of the king's women. These virgins would not be simply participating in a beauty pageant but would undergo a year of training, purification, and beautification. Six months with myrrh and six with exotic perfumes. All this prior to going before the king.

Harems were separate palaces within the royal enclosure where the ruler's wives, concubines and children lived—even the boys until they were sixteen years old. The harem, which means "safe place," was a well-ordered society and often ruled by the monarch's mother. Chamberlains, who were eunuchs, provided security. The women were taught to read and write with a view to perhaps securing a secretarial position in the royal household. Harems were not brothels.

As each of the virgin's turn came, she would go before the king in the evening, taking anything that she wished from the harem. In the morning she would be returned to the harem where the concubines stayed and would not return to the king unless he was pleased enough with her to summon her by name.

Esther, whose Jewish name was Hadassah, was an orphaned Jewish girl who had been brought up by her cousin, Mordecai. Mordecai had intended to take Esther as his wife, but when the royal decree was issued, Esther, who was uncommonly beautiful, was installed in the harem to await her turn to go before the king.

Esther is a Persian name which means "star." Hadassah means "myrtle," an evergreen tree with dark glossy leaves and fragrant white flowers.

Mordecai, who was a functionary at the palace, went to the gates of the harem every day and spoke with the guards to ensure that Esther was in good health and spirits.

After a year of preparation, which happened to be in the seventh year of Xerxes's reign, Esther was summoned to the king's chamber. It was her turn. Just imagine the beautiful music of Scheherazade (Esther's voice) as she spoke to her king and sense the aroma of her exotic perfumes. King Xerxes fell head over heels for her and placed the queen's crown on her head.

Even though Esther was now the queen and therefore Xerxes's favorite wife, she could not come and go at will to the king's court—she had to be summoned. The penalty for overlooking this stricture was death.

One day Mordecai overheard two of the palace guards, Bigthan and Teresh, who were part of the king's bodyguard, plotting regicide. Mordecai reported the plot to Esther, who duly passed it on to her husband in Mordecai's name.

Xerxes immediately launched an investigation, and upon the pairs' confession under interrogation, had them executed. Mordecai received a commendation, which was entered into the royal archives.

One prince of the realm was Haman, an Agagite, who was a favorite of Xerxes. Haman was violently anti-Semitic. Generations earlier, Agag had been executed by the prophet Samuel, during the reign of King Saul. Haman held the rank of prime minister. Haman was very upset over the deaths of Bigthan and Teresh, and he determined to avenge them, and having found that Mordecai was Jewish, he decided to turn the king against Mordecai and all the Jews in the kingdom. Haman offered to pay ten thousand talents of silver into the treasury, presumably to help defray the costs of the proposed purge. Xerxes declined the offer.

Because of Haman's high rank, people were required to bow to him whenever they passed him. Mordecai never did so. Haman went to the king and told him that there was a large segment of the population within the kingdom who worshipped a different God and were actively disloyal to Xerxes. Haman proposed the extermination of these people once and for all and cast lots to decide which day the plan should be put into effect.

King Xerxes gave his approval of the plan and wrote a proclamation to the princes and governors of all the provinces of his kingdom—that on the fourteenth day of the twelfth month, every Jewish person—man, woman, and child shall be put to death.

When he learned of the order, Mordecai "rent his clothes and wore sackcloth and ashes." Esther, not understanding the reason for her cousin's behavior, sent her servant, Achrathaeus, with new clothes for him to wear. Mordecai refused to wear them. Mordecai showed Achrathaeus the letter ordering the slaughter and bade him take it to the queen and beg her to intercede with the king.

Queen Esther laid aside her royal apparel, wore sackcloth, ashes, and dung. She fasted for three days and prayed for strength and deliverance.

After three days, Esther dressed in her royal clothes and went unbidden into the king's court. At first Xerxes was angry at the intrusion, but when he saw that it was Esther, he held out his scepter for her to touch.

The king asked Esther what she wanted, "for whatever thy request, even up to half of the kingdom, it shall be given thee." She replied that she had prepared a banquet for Haman and asked the king to attend. Xerxes ordered Haman to attend Esther's banquet. During the feast, the king again asked the nature of Esther's petition and again offered half the kingdom. Esther asked that he and Haman attend another banquet that she was giving the next day.

Haman went home, consumed with happiness that the king and queen though so highly of him. He boasted of his riches and power to his wife, Zeresh. But in his stomach, Mordecai's refusal to bow to him burned like acid. Zeresh and Haman's friends decided to build a gallows of fifty cubits in height to hang Mordecai on.

On the night before Esther's banquet, Xerxes suffered from a bout of insomnia and ordered that the book of records be read to him. When the chamberlain came to the passage concerning Bigthan and Teresh, the king asked what honor and dignity had been bestowed on

Mordecai for his fealty. The chamberlain replied that nothing had been done for him.

The king then enquired as to who was in the king's court. The servant said that Haman had come to speak with the king about hanging Mordecai on his new gallows. The king said to the chamberlain, "Let him come in."

So Haman entered the inner court, and the king asked him what should be done for a man whom the king delights to honor? Haman thought to himself, *Who would the king delight to honor besides me?*

Haman replied that such a man should be dressed in some of the king's clothing and ride on one of the king's horses. Horse and rider should be led by one of the noble princes of the land who will proclaim, "Thus it shall be done to the man whom the king is delighted to honor."

Xerxes ordered Haman to hasten to Mordecai, the Jew, taking the clothes and the horse to him and do exactly what he had suggested. Haman did as he was bidden, arraying Mordecai in the royal garments and leading him and the horse through the streets of Shushan and making the agreed proclamation.

Mordecai returned to the king's gate, but Haman hurried home sorely troubled, and with his head covered. Upon telling Zeresh and his friends what had befallen him, Zeresh said, "If Mordecai, before whom thou hast begun to fall, be of the seed of the Jews, thou shalt not prevail against him, but shalt surely fall before him."

As this conversation was taking place, the king's chamberlains arrived to escort him to the queen's banquet, at which Xerxes gave the house of Haman to Esther. Mordecai appeared before the king, and Esther told her husband of her relationship to Mordecai.

The king took off the ring that he had taken from Haman and gave it to Mordecai, and Esther set her cousin over the house of Haman. Xerxes stepped outside into the orchard for a breath of air. Haman threw himself at Esther's feet, begging for his life. The king returned and thought that Haman was assaulting Esther. Haman was dragged away to his doom.

Esther prostrated herself before the king, begging him to reverse Haman's genocidal plan to which he had given his blessing earlier. Xerxes held out his scepter to Esther and said that Haman had been hanged on his own gallows but that he was unable to reverse the order to kill all the Jews, but what he could do was to give orders that the Jews could band together and resist any that came against them and take the spoils of war. Mordecai left the palace wearing robes of blue and white and wearing a golden crown.

The city of Shushan rejoiced. In the provinces, the Jews feasted, and many gentiles converted to Judaism for fear of being attacked by the Jews.

As the day of the king's decree, the thirteenth day of Adar, the twelfth month approached, the princes and governors assisted the Jews out of fear of Mordecai who was now King Xerxes's prime minister. The Jews slaughtered all that came against them, killing 75,000 of their enemies but declined to take any spoils.

Esther declared that these days shall be called *Purim* and were to be celebrated annually. And so they are to this day.

Purim is celebrated annually on the fourteenth day of the Hebrew month of Adar, the day following the victory of the Jews over their enemies. Purim begins at sundown on the previous secular day. In cities that were protected by walls at the time of Joshua, including Shushan and Jerusalem, Purim is celebrated on the fifteenth of the month, known as *Shushan Purim.*

Purim is characterized by public recitation of the book of Esther, giving mutual gifts of food and drink, giving charity to the poor and a celebratory meal. Every time Haman's name is mentioned, a gragger, which is a noisy rattle, is used to blot out evil.

Source: The Septuagint: Book of Esther

THE MAGDALENE

Why do I not love you like her? When a blind man and one who sees are both together in darkness, they are no different from one another. When the light comes, then he who sees will see the light, and he who is blind will remain in darkness.

Jesus Christ
Gospel of Philip

The Bible refers to her as Mary *Magdalene* in order to differentiate her from the other women named Mary. She is also referred to as the Apostles' Apostle, and the beloved disciple. It is thought that she came from Magdala, a town on the western shore of the Sea of Galilee. Luke (8:2) says that she was actually called *Magdalene*. In Aramaic, *magdala* means "tower," or "elevated, great, magnificent." Any or all of these epithets fit this great woman perfectly.

Magdalene had led such a virtuous and chaste life that Satan thought that she would be the mother of Jesus Christ and consequently afflicted her with seven demons. When Jesus exorcised the demons, she became his constant companion, lover, and most important disciple.

During Jesus' ministry in Galilee, his entourage included several other women disciples, besides

Magdalene: his mother, Mary, Joanna, Susanna, and Salome, to name a few who "provided for Him from their own subsidence." (Luke 8:2, 3)

Many of the other disciples, particularly Peter, were very envious of Mary's close relationship with Jesus. Simon Peter said to them: "Let Mary go forth from among us, for women are not worthy of the life." Jesus said, "Behold, I shall lead her that I may make her male, in order that she also may become a living spirit like you males. For every woman who makes herself male shall enter into the kingdom of heaven" (Gospel of Thomas).

Magdalene frequently had to explain some of Jesus' teachings to the other disciples. Jesus said to her, "Mary, thou blessed one, whom I will perfect in all mysteries of those of the height, discourse in openness, thou, whose heart is raised to the kingdom of heaven more than all thy brethren."

Magdalene stayed with Jesus until the end. She was there with him during his trial before Pontius Pilate, the Roman prefect of Judea, his scourging, and his crucifixion. Most of the other disciples went into hiding, but not this woman. She attended Jesus' burial and was the first to go down to the tomb of the garden, armed with oils and ointments to anoint her beloved Jesus' body, only to find that the tomb was open and Jesus' body was gone.

She stood outside the tomb, weeping tears of frustration, that she had been denied the opportunity to perform this last service to her Lord. As she wept, a person whom she took to be a gardener approached and asked, "Why are you crying?"

Mary asked the man if he knew where the body had been taken because she was prepared to go and get Jesus herself and bring him back to the tomb. Then the man addressed her by name, and she knew it was the resurrected Jesus. Thus, she was the first witness to the resurrection.

Following Mary's recognition of the risen Jesus, Peter came out of hiding and declared that Mary was not to be believed because she was a woman and that her testimony was therefore suspect. Peter and some of the other disciples decided to assert themselves and take the leadership of Christianity from her and, shortly after, started the malicious slander of Magdalene's reputation as a reformed prostitute.

The Easter egg tradition stems from Magdalene. She was invited to a banquet given by the Emperor Tiberius. She held a plain egg in her hand and showed to it Tiberius exclaiming, "Christ is risen!" Caesar scoffed and said Christ rising from the dead was as likely as the egg in Mary's hand turning red. Before he had finished speaking, the egg turned bright red. Another version of this story is that Magdalene and the Virgin Mary placed a basket of eggs at the foot of the cross after the crucifixion, and the eggs were painted red by Christ's blood and Magdalene took them to Tiberius.

Sources: Holy Bible. New King James Version

The Septuagint

The Golden Legend or Lives of the
Saints Vol IV Jacobus de Voragine

BOADICEA: WARRIOR QUEEN OF BRITANNIA

She was most tall, in the glance of her eye most fierce, her voice harsh. A great mass of the reddest hair fell down to her hips. Her appearance was terrifying.

Cassius Dio, Roman historian

Her name takes many forms in many manuscripts; the modern form from the late twentieth century is Boudicca. Tacitus, the renowned Roman historian of this time, took a particular interest in Britannia, as his father-in-law was a military tribune who had served three tours of duty there. He refers to her as Boadicea, which was as she was called during my studies as a schoolboy in England. Dio also paid her a left-handed compliment: "She was possessed of greater intelligence than often belongs to women."

The name in any of its versions means "victory" or "victorious." This great woman of history enjoyed a resurgence of popularity during the reign of Queen Victoria for obvious reasons. Lord Tennyson, Victoria's poet laureate, wrote a poem "Boadicea," and several naval ships and bases were named after her. Prince

Albert commissioned a bronze statue of her with her children in a war chariot. The statue, executed by Thomas Thornycroft, stands next to Westminster Bridge and the Houses of Parliament, with the following lines from William Cowper's poem referring to the British Empire:

Boadicea: an ode;

"Regions Caesar never knew

Thy posterity shall sway"

Ironically, Boadicea stands guard over London, a city which she once razed to ground.

In the first century AD, The Iceni tribe occupied a large area of East Anglia in what is roughly Norfolk today. Britannia was Rome's most recent province. Britannia was acquired by the force of Roman arms during the reign of Emperor Claudius (41–54 AD).

The king of the Iceni was Prasutagus, who was a Roman "client king."

Roman client kingdoms were native tribes that chose to align themselves with the Roman Empire because they saw it as a good option for protection against hostile tribes. The Romans, for their part, enlisted some tribes when they felt that influence without direct rule to be desirable. Today we would think of such an arrangement as a "two-way street." The normal practice was to allow these kingdoms their independence only for the lifetime of their kings, who would agree to bequeath their kingdoms to Rome upon their deaths. Roman law only allowed inheritance through the male line.

This client-king arrangement worked very well for Prasutagus and the Iceni, and he lived a long and prosperous life, but when he died, he had attempted to make the emperor (Nero) co-heir to his kingdom along with his wife and two daughters.

His wishes were ignored, his kingdom annexed, as though it had been conquered. His lands were confiscated, and his nobles treated as slaves. Tacitus tells us that the queen was flogged and her daughters raped.

At the time, the Roman governor of Britannia, Suetonius, was attempting to subdue the island of Mona (Anglesey), in north Wales. Mona was a refuge for British rebels and a stronghold for the Druids.

The Roman army in Britannia, then, consisted of four legions: the XIV (*Gemina*) and the XX (*Valeria Victrix*), which were with Suetonius in North Wales; the IX (*Hispana*) was in Lincoln, and the II *(Augusta) at* Gloucester.

The Iceni joined forces with a neighboring tribe, the Trinovantes, to revolt. The Trinovantes' ancestors had driven Julius Caesar himself from the British shores. Boadicea was chosen as their leader. She released a hare from the folds of her robe and interpreted the direction in which ran as a divination.

No one knows for sure which way the hare darted, but it was likely in the direction of Camulodunum (Colchester), as that city turned out to be the first target of Boadicea and her army. Camulodunum was the former Trinovantian capital, but it was now a Roman colonia. Roman army veterans who settled there treated the local inhabitants badly, and a temple to Claudius was built there at local expense. The Roman inhabitants asked for military aid from the procurator Decianus, but he only sent two hundred auxiliary troops.

Boadicea's army assaulted the city and destroyed it. They laid siege to the temple, which held the last of the defenders for two days before it fell. The city was methodically demolished. The IX Legion, under the command of Quintas Petillius, attempted to relieve the city but suffered an overwhelming defeat. The infantry was annihilated, but Petillius was able to flee with the remnants of his cavalry. Decianus fled to Gaul.

When news of the rebellion reached Suetonius, he hurried along Watling Street, through hostile territory, to Londinium (London), a relatively new town which had become a thriving trading center, with a population of travelers, traders, and Roman officials. Suetonius thought of giving battle there, but considering his small numbers and the defeat of IX Legion, he decided to sacrifice Londinium in order to save the province.

Abandoned, Londinium was put to the torch, and any that had not fled with Suetonius were put to the sword

Boadicea's next target was the city of Verulanium (St. Albans), which was similarly burnt to the ground, with much slaughter and barbarism, and according to Dio, "to the accompaniment of sacrifices, banquets, and wanton behavior in sacred places." The "sacred places" being the Groves of Andraste, the British goddess of victory.

The Battle of Watling Street

Suetonius regrouped with the XIV Legion and elements of the XX. The prefect of the II Legion ignored his call, but Suetonius was able to put about 10,000 men in the field. He was also able to pick the site of the battle, a distinct military advantage, and he chose well—the battlefield near Watling Street, possibly in the West Midlands. He took up a position at the head of a defile with a forest behind him, which ensured that his small army could not be surrounded by Boadicea's superior force, said to number 230,000. This number is probably an exaggeration, but she was certainly far superior in numbers to the Romans.

Boadicea exhorted her troops from her chariot, her daughters beside her, declaring that if men wanted to live in slavery, it was their choice to do so, but that she as a woman was resolved to win or die.

Because of Suetonius's choice of battlefield, the Britons were only able to engage the Romans on a narrow front and could not envelope them. The Britons charged, and the Romans cut them down by the thousand with volleys of their heavy javelins. Having used up their javelins, the Romans advanced in wedge formation, using their short stabbing swords. The Britons attempted to flee but were impeded by their own wagons, which were drawn up in a semicircle around the battlefield and were slaughtered. Tacitus reports that 80,000 Britons were killed, compared to 400 Roman soldiers.

Boadicea took poison and was accorded a lavish funeral. Legend has it that she is buried under what is now number ten platform at King's Cross Station in London.

Suetoniusl for his part took violent punitive action against the British, but criticism of this policy from Rome halted the violence. And Suetonius was replaced by Publius

Petronius. The crisis had almost persuaded Nero to abandon Britannia, as he did not want to have a wasteland for a province.

As a footnote, sightings of Boadicea and her chariot, dating back to the mid-nineteenth century, have been reported in Lincolnshire. Many a traveler and motorist have spotted her riding to some unknown destination.

Lesson: Do not allow yourself to be downtrodden. Always stand tall.

Sources: Churchill: History of the
English Speaking People

Roman Military Research Society

DAHIA AL-KAHINA: WARRIOR AND SOOTHSAYER

Kahina's name in classical Arabic means "female seer," and her Muslim opponents gave her that soubriquet because of her reputed ability to foresee the future. She is thought to have resided in the Aures Mountains, an extension of the Atlas Mountains of eastern Algeria. These mountains served as a refuge for Berber tribes, forming a base of resistance against such invaders as the Romans, Vandals, and Arabs. She was born in the early seventh century and died at the ripe old age of 127 years. She was possibly the leader of the Jrawa tribe.

She was thought by nineteenth century historians to have been Jewish, but since she always carried an "idol" on her travels, possibly of the Virgin Mary, she was much more likely to have been a Christian. Further, oral legends of Algerian Jews describe her as an ogress and persecutor of Jews.

She could have been of mixed descent: Berber and Byzantine Christian, especially as one of her three sons was Greek.

Of the many legends of Kahina, a number of them comment on her long hair and great size, and the fact that she had three sons pointed to the possibility that she was a sorceress. These being the characteristics of witches in legends. One her sons was adopted; he was an Arab officer whom she had captured during one of her campaigns.

Another legend claims that the young Kahina freed her people by marrying a tyrant and then murdering him on their wedding night.

The encroaching Arab armies of the Umayyad Dynasty, under the command of Hasan ibn al-Nu'man, marched from Egypt and captured the city of Carthage. Searching for another enemy to defeat, he was told that the most powerful monarch in North Africa was Kahina, queen of the Berbers. So he and his army marched into Numidia. Numidia was the area between Tunisia and Morocco, with the Mediterranean Sea to the north and the Sahara to the south.

The armies met near Meskiana, in the present day province of Oum el Bouaghi, Algeria. Kahina defeated Hasan so completely that he fled to Cyrenaica and stayed there for five years. Kahina realized that the enemy was too powerful not to return. She embarked on a scorched earth policy, which lost for her the crucial support of the sedentary oasis dwellers. Instead of discouraging the Arab armies, her desperate and unwise strategy hastened her defeat.

Hasan eventually returned and, aided by communications with Kahina's adopted son, the former Arab officer, defeated her in Algeria. Kahina foresaw the outcome of the battle and sent her two natural sons over to the Arab army in the care of her adopted one. Hasan gave one of them command of a section of his forces.

Kahina died fighting the invaders, sword in hand, a warrior's death.

In later centuries, her legend was used to bolster the claims of the Berbers in Moorish Spain against the Arab claim of ethnic supremacy. Her name was also invoked by French colonials, Berber nationalists, Arab Nationalists, North African Jews, North African feminists, and Maghrebi nationalists alike for their own didactic purposes.

Source: Ronuko Rashidi: Dahia Al-Kahina
Valiant North African Freedom Fighter

GODIVA:
NAKED COURAGE

Frequently referred to as Lady Godiva, she was actually an Anglo-Saxon noblewoman, whose husband was Leofric, earl of Mercia. Her name in Old English, *Godgifu*, means "gift of God." Both she and Leofric were generous benefactors to religious establishments. In fact, Leofric founded and endowed a Benedictine monastery at Coventry in Warwickshire, although Godiva is credited as being the driving force behind this deed.

They gave St. Paul's Cathedral on Ludgate Hill in London a life-size gold and silver crucifix and a valuable necklace to be hung round the neck of the Virgin. Note that this cathedral was not Sir Christopher Wren's masterpiece but one of the early churches built on the same site. She and her husband were among the most generous of the Anglo-Saxon donors prior to the Norman Conquest (1066 AD).

Following the conquest, the early Norman bishops lost no time in pilfering many of the donations and scuttled back to Normandy with the booty or melted it down for bullion.

The people of Coventry were burdened with onerous taxation imposed by Leofric. Time and again,

Godiva appealed to her husband to lighten the load, until one day Leofric told his wife that he would accede to her requests if she would ride through the town naked. Lady Godiva took him at his word and, after ordering that everyone should stay indoors and shutter their windows, rode through the town clad in only her long hair.

The story goes that a tailor bored a hole in one of his shutters so as not to miss the show.

Forever after, he has been known as *Peeping Tom*. He was struck blind, which couldn't have helped his tailoring business very much—an infamous instance of voyeurism.

Leofric kept his word and abolished the heavy taxation.

Other versions of the legend have Godiva riding through Coventry with the population lining the street, or only wearing a slip, or stripped of her jewelry.

Sources: Churchill: History of the
English Speaking People

ST. JOAN OF ARC: LA PUCELLE D'ORLEANS

There now appeared upon the ravaged scene an Angel of Deliverance, the noblest patriot of France, the most splendid of her heroes, the most beloved of her saints, the most inspiring of all her memories, the peasant Maid, the ever-shining, ever-glorious Joan of Arc.

Winston S. Churchill,
A History of the English Speaking Peoples

If Joan isn't the greatest woman that ever walked on this planet, she is certainly in the top twenty.

Joan was born in 1412 in the small village of Domremy and was burned at the stake, in Rouen, in 1431. Her parents were Jacques d'Arc and Isabelle Romee. Joan was the youngest of five siblings, three brothers—Jacquemin, Little-Jean, and Pierre, and a sister, Catherine. Joan was born during the celebration of Epiphany, and legend has it that the local cockerels crowed at midnight.

At this time, the Hundred Years War, which was started when England's King Edward III laid claim to the crown of France, had been raging on and off for eighty years. Now that King Henry V had married Catherine of Valois, he had become the regent of

France and, under the Treaty of Troyes, would become king upon the death of French King Charles VI who was insane. Charles's queen, Isabeau, had been acting for him in all matters of State. Queen Isabeau was promiscuous to say the least and had even claimed that her own son, the heir apparent or dauphin, Charles, was illegitimate in order to bolster Henry's claim. Matters came to a head when Isabeau's lover, the Duke of Orleans, was murdered shortly after leaving the queen's bed. It transpired that the murderer was the Duke of Burgundy, John the Fearless, a cruel and lawless man who had always hated his urbane cousin.

Thus France was now split into two warring factions—the Burgundians, followers of Jean the Fearless and collaborators of the English, and the Armagnacs, supporters of the Dauphin Charles and opponents of the English.

Joan's village of Domremy lay nestled on the left bank of the River Meuse. The summit of the hill behind the village belonged to the Duke of Bar (later annexed to the province of Lorraine and renamed Domremy-la-Pucelle) with Anglo-Burgundian sympathies. Only the valley and the river which flowed through it belonged to the king of France.

Jacques d'Arc owned about fifty acres of land which he farmed, raised cattle, sheep, and horses. He supplemented his income as a local tax collector and headed the local watch.

Isabelle instructed her children in the faith and the lessons of the commandments, as well as household chores, sewing, and spinning. She gave special attention to Joan and her sisters because of their being more tempting to the devil on account of their innocence. According to Joan, the idea that she was a shepherdess was a myth, as she said, "I worked at common household tasks and went seldom to the fields with our sheep and other cattle."

Myths and legends abounded among the simple peasant folk of Domremy. There was a large beech tree in the middle of the village that was considered to have magical powers, and the villagers danced round it at certain times of the year. Ailing people were known to have been healed by it. There was also a mandrake on the outskirts of the village under a nut tree, which the villagers feared because of its aphrodisiacal powers. The plant was said to flourish at the foot of gallows. Visible from the d'Arcs' home was a dark forbidding forest known as the Bois Chenu, which the villagers avoided after nightfall, as all kinds of forbidding spirits were thought to haunt it.

One legend that the villagers did not know about the forest because it was not until 1429 that Armagnac clerks began circulating a prediction, citing Merlin as the prophet:

> From the place of Bois Chenu will come a maid who will give her care to healing and who, after throwing down all citadels will dry up all fountains with her breath. ...she will be slain by the stag with ten antlers of which four branches will bear crowns of gold, but of which six will be changed to buffalo horns that will trouble the isles of Britain with a woeful sound.
>
> Ditie de Jehanne d' Arc. Catherine de Pizan
Prophecy of The Venerable Bede

Joan started hearing her voices when she was thirteen. They came from a dazzling burst of sunlight. At first it was the voice of St. Michael, and Joan was very frightened, but later St Michael came with Saints. Margaret and Catherine, whose voices were both beautiful and soothing. They told her that she must maintain a state of absolute purity, and she vowed to keep her virginity "for as long as it should please God."

The saints told her that Charles must be restored to his kingdom, and as soon as possible, and that she must raise the siege of Orleans. As times grew worse, the saints became more urgent with her instructions. In return they said that they would lead her into paradise. She pleaded that she knew nothing of the conduct of wars, but they assured her God would give her explicit instructions.

Although eager to obey, she was filled with apprehension, lest the Burgundians found out and would prevent her. But most of all, she feared that her father would never allow her to leave the house except as bride. Jacques told Isabelle that he had a recurring dream that Joan had run off with a band of soldiers. Isabelle told Joan that only harlots followed soldiers.

Joan knew that she had to go to Vaucouleurs and see Robert de Baudricourt, the captain of the royal garrison there, and ask him to give her some men to take her to see the Dauphin. But what scheme could she cook up that her father would let out of the house for a few nights and not arouse suspicion? There was one person who Joan could wrap around her little finger and could trust to keep her secret: Durand Lassois, her cousin Jeanne's husband. Joan called him "Uncle Lassois" in deference to his age of thirty-eight years.

If Uncle Lassois had any misgivings about the mission, Joan's intensity caused him to quickly put them aside. She asked him, "Haven't you heard it said that France, ruined through a woman, would be restored by a girl from the borders of Lorraine?" She left him to guess who that girl might be.

Another young woman who had visions, Marie, the maid of Avignon, had been sent to Charles VI by Pope Benedict XIII to "keep him in the Holy Father's obedience." Marie also advised the king that as bad as things were in France, conditions were going to get a lot worse. In her visions, her heavenly hosts showed her a suit of armor that made her tremble with fear, but they consoled her with the knowledge that another maid would be wearing it and drive out the enemy.

Joan and Durand set out on foot for Vaucouleurs. She wore a much-mended red dress of coarse material, with her hair concealed by a bandana, as custom dictated. As they trudged along, Durand must have worried about the reception that they would receive from Baudricourt. They behavior of nobles was uncertain, especially toward peasants.

Arriving at Baudricourt's reception hall, Joan walked right up to the captain who was indistinguishable from the soldiers who were with him in the room and said, "I am come to you on behalf of Messire (God) that you send a message to the Dauphin to refrain from of engaging in battle with his enemies." Baudricourt and his soldiers were amused at this peasant girl's statement, and the Dauphin, had he been there to hear it, would have been delighted with it, as he had no urge to get involved with fighting whatever. Joan embarrassed and realizing that she had only delivered a part of the message, recovered her composure and added, "Before mid-lent Messire will give him succor."

The soldiers glanced at each other and made lewd remarks. Joan continued, "Indeed the kingdom of France is not the Dauphin's but Messire's. But Messire wills that the Dauphin shall be made king and hold the kingdom in his custody. In spite of his enemies the Dauphin will be king and I shall lead him to his coronation." The soldiers, mirthful before, were now rolling in the aisles, except for Bertrand de Poulengy who took Joan seriously. The thought crossed Baudricourt's mind to have his soldiers "skirmish with her in sin." Durand now plucked courage to support Joan's plea, Baudricourt turned to him and told him, curtly, to take her back to her father for a sound spanking.

Back home again, Joan had to explain things to her irate father, as her interview with Robert de Baudricourt had become common knowledge. The villagers wondered if she had become a little "touched" by the spirits which haunted Bois Chenu or had associated with the fairies under the beech tree.

On the sixth of January, 1429, Joan was seventeen years old. It had been nine months since she had been to see Baudricourt, and she decided that she could delay her mission no longer. Durand's wife was nearing her confinement, and under normal circumstances, Joan would be helping out round the house. Instead she and Uncle Lassois planned a second foray to see Robert de Baudricourt. It is remarkable that when Durand came calling for Joan, her parents fell for it again. Together they set out for Vaucouleurs.

Joan presented herself at the castle and stated boldly, "My lord Captain, again and again, God has commanded me to go to the gracious Dauphin who must be and is the true king of France. And he, the dauphin, is to furnish me with soldiers so I may raise the siege of Orleans and lead him to Reims to be anointed."

Baudricourt did not laugh at her this time. He was impressed with her sincerity and wondered how an ignorant peasant girl would know about the siege of Orleans and the feuds over the crown of France. Of one thing he was certain: the kingdom of France had never been in graver peril, but yet he did not offer to assist her.

Bertrand de Poulengy had won over his friend known as Jean de Metz, another professional soldier. So Joan now had an entourage of three—two soldiers and Uncle Lassois, and Lassois managed to recruit a young man in the town. Lassois and Alain bought Joan a horse and fitted her out with male clothing.

Joan received an invitation from the duke of Lorraine and a safe-conduct to Nancy. It was a journey of some twenty-five miles. So with Joan mounted and Uncle Lassois and Alain walking, the trio set off to see the duke. The duke actually wanted Joan to cure him of VD, but she was quick to deny any knowledge of medicine and gave him a lecture on immorality instead. That did not exactly please his lordship, but he thanked her for the advice and gave her four francs and a black horse.

It was on the twelfth of February that Baudricourt learned of the disastrous outcome of the Battle of Rouvray, which came to be known as the Battle of the Herrings in which the French army attacked an English supply column and got soundly thrashed. They did manage to damage some casks of salt fish, which were going to the English troops besieging Orleans.

By coincidence Charles VII's messenger, Colet de Vienne, arrived at Vaucouleurs with instructions to lead Joan to Chinon. The vacillating king had finally made a sound decision to interview Joan. After all, nothing else had worked, so why not fly in the face of military doctrine and put this peasant girl at the head of his army?

The townspeople of Vaucouleurs passed the hat round to raise some cash and to outfit Joan for her trip halfway across France, through enemy territory. They bought her a better horse and a smart male outfit. Baudricourt gave her a sword. So on the twenty-third of February, Joan, accompanied by Colet de Vienne, Jean de Metz, and Poulengy with their two servants and an archer named Richard. Joan in her dark grey tunic, black doublet, hose and boots, proudly wearing her sword, set off for Chinon. Lassois and Alain returned to their homes.

At last on the sixth of March, La Pucelle and her little party entered Chinon. Joan went straight to the king and fell at his feet and embraced his knees. The men of the court greatly admired her beauty, as she was still wearing her traveling suit hand the tight-fitting hose showed her thighs off to advantage. The women of that licentious court wondered why with all her advantages she was the maid of God. Charles drew her to her feet after she had repeated her reason for coming. She also told him that, "I shall last a year, perhaps a little longer, therefore let us set ourselves to do good work in that year."

Charles wanted a sign, so he sent her to Poitiers to be examined by scholars and churchmen, to be sure that she was a woman and a virgin and not in league with Satan.

The worthies at Poitiers gave Joan a clean bill of health—"A virgin true and entire."

"I did not come to Poitiers to perform prodigies! Send me to Orleans. Then I'll show you the miracles I've been sent to perform. Give me as many soldiers as you see fit, and I promise to raise the siege of that city."

The king and his advisors agreed to send Joan with supplies to the beleaguered city. She assured them that none would come out to contest the delivery. Joan, whom as we know was illiterate and could not sign her name unless her hand was held, asked for scribes as she dictated a letter to the infant King Henry VI and his senior military commanders lords Bedford, Suffolk, Talbot, and Scales, of which the following is the gist:

"King of England, and you, Duke of Bedford, who call yourself regent of the kingdom of France…settle your debt to the king of Heaven, return to the Maiden, who is the envoy of the king of Heaven, the keys to all the good towns you took and violated in France."

Now after months of setbacks, the vacillations of king and dukes, she was about to go about God's work. She was equipped with a suit of white armor and a standard of her own design—a white field sown with lilies and fringed with silk and bearing the motto—*Jhesus*

Maria. She also requested a sword that her voices had told her of. The Dauphin sent an armorer to the church of St. Catherine where the voices had told her it would be found. He found it and was staggered as the rust fell away and it shone as new.

Imagine that day, April 27, 1429, a beautiful peasant girl resplendent in shining white armor, banner unfurled, riding at the head of an army three thousand strong, with priests leading the way into Blois, chanting *Veni Creator,* her faithful escorts from Vaucouleurs at her side.

The next day the army reached the heights of Olivet, about two miles from Orleans. As she looked down, she could see the positions of the besieging English forces across the Loire. She wondered, angrily, what she and her army were doing on opposite sides of the river. The natural son of the duke of Orleans, known as the Bastard of Orleans, came up the river by boat to greet her, but Joan was in no mood for niceties and complained that he should have led her directly to Talbot and the English.

A favorable change in the wind which Joan had predicted enabled the bastard's men to load the supplies which Joan had brought onto barges out of sight of the English. She and her army rested overnight at the village of Chechy before riding on to the city.

The English army, under the command of the Dukes Bedford and Talbot, made no move to intercept the French. There were gaps in the English encirclement, particularly between the fortresses of St. Loup and St. Pouair. The Bastard had been smuggling in supplies all along through this gap.

On the twenty-ninth of April, Joan of Arc and the French army entered Orleans. The whole city turned out rejoicing, and many people endeavored to touch La Pucelle. But all was not well, as some of the captains of the French army resented Joan's presence and obvious authority, and they excluded her from their councils.

On May 4, she stormed and captured the outlying fortress of Saint Loup. The next day she followed with an attack on fortress Saint Jean le Blanc, which was found to be deserted.

The next day she opposed the Bastard's plan to seek further reinforcements, and she demanded another assault on the enemy. He, on his part, ordered the gates of the city to be locked. But she, with aid of the townspeople and her soldiers, forced the mayor to unlock a gate. With the aid of only one captain and her common soldiers, she rode out and captured the fortress of St. Augustins. That evening she discovered that she had been excluded from a meeting where the leaders had decided on yet more reinforcements before acting again. She insisted on assaulting main English stronghold of Les Tourelles.

On May 7, she did exactly that and, despite being wounded in the neck by an English arrow while climbing a scaling ladder and had to the helped to the rear, came back and led the French army to another great victory.

La Pucelle's next plan was to capture the bridges across the Loire as a prelude to an advance on Reims and the coronation of Charles VII. It was a daring proposal because Reims was twice as far away as Paris and deep in enemy territory. Joan asked permission from

Charles VII to grant her co-command of the army with Duke John II of Alencon.

On the eleventh of June, the army captured Jargeau; on the fifteenth, Meung-sue-Loire, then Beaugency on the seventeenth. Alencon credited Joan with saving his life at Jargeau by telling him, "Step aside. Step aside. You are in danger." Just as he complied, a cannon ball struck the spot where he had been standing.

On June 18, an English relief force, under Sir John Fastolf, arrived on the scene. Alencon wanted to rest before taking on Fastolf at Panay. Joan would have none of it, and the French attacked Panay. If the rout of the English had been a slaughter before, it was now a bloody carnage, and Panay was Agincourt in reverse. The French vanguard attacked before the English archers with their famous long bows could set up and a rout ensued. Both Suffolk and Talbot were taken prisoner. Bedford was so angry at Fastolf that he stripped him of the Order of the Garter.

Joan's army set out for Reims from Gien-sur-Loire on June 29. Charles, dragging along behind the army, joined her division at the gates to the Burgundian city of Auxerre. Charles wrote to the citizens of Auxerre demanding their unconditional surrender. This, they unconditionally refused to do. La Pucelle herself wrote numerous letters, one to the citizens of Tournai:

"…the Maiden lets you know that in eight days, she has chased the English out of all the places they held on the river Loire by attack or other means: they are dead or prisoners or discouraged in battle. Believe what you have heard about the Earl of Suffolk, the lord la Pole and his brother,

the Lord Talbot, the lord Scales, and Sir Fastolf, many more knights and captains than these are defeated."

From July 5 until July 11, the French army stood before Troyes, the city where the infamous Treaty had been signed disinheriting Charles. The citizens of Troyes expected the same terms of surrender as those of Auxerre. The sneaky Archbishop of Reims tried to have the siege discontinued. Ramon le Macon, former Chancellor of the realm, spoke out saying that Joan should be consulted on the situation before any decision was made. Joan entered the council and asked if her words would be believed, Charles hedged and said it depended what she had to say.

Joan said, "Gentil Dauphin, order your people to advance on Troyes. For in God's name, I will bring you into Troyes, by valor, force, or favor before three days have passed."

That night, Joan personally supervised the placing the cannon and the culverin and setting up towers against the walls. The next morning, the anxious people of Troyes saw flashing steel and Joan's white banner fluttering in the breeze. That was enough for them; they sent out a party to capitulate. The weakling Charles accepted their surrender and took it as his personal victory.

She said during an interview with two visitors from Domremy at this time that, "I fear nothing but treachery." Did she have some inkling of what was going on behind her back between high officials of the church and some of Charles's sycophants?

Reims opened its gates, and Charles was crowned the next day, July 16. Joan and Alencon urged a prompt

march on Paris, but the ever-hesitant royal court nego-
tiated a truce with the duke of Burgundy. Duke Philip
the Good used the truce as a stalling tactic to reinforce
Paris' defenses. The French army assaulted Paris on
September, and despite a crossbow quarrel wound to
the leg, Joan continued to direct her troops until the
end of the day's fighting. Then she received a royal
order to withdraw. More bungling and treachery in
high places. This political gaffe is blamed on Georges
de la Tremoille, the French grand chamberlain.

In October she took Saint-Pierre-le Mousier and
was ennobled by the king.

After spending the winter of 1429 wandering
unhappily and uselessly in Charles' court, she grasped
at an opportunity for action. She attempted to raise the
siege of Compiegne. But she no longer had her trusted
lieutenants, or even a decent force, and was forced to
order a retreat. She was the last fall back and she was
captured.

Normally she would have been held for ransom,
but her family was poor and the weak-willed king did
nothing to help her. She made numerous attempts at
escape, once even leaping seventy feet from a window
in the tower where she was imprisoned. The English
government eventually bought her, and her trial for
heresy was soon forthcoming.

Joan was summoned to appear before her judges
"on Wednesday the 21st of February, at eight o'clock in
the morning in the chapel royal of the Castle to answer
to a questioning...under pain of excommunication."

And so in the early morning of February 21, 1431,
Joan stepped into the light of day for the first time in

nearly three months, to take part in the *processus ordinarius* of the inquisitorial drama.

The examiners, forty-two of them, theologians, archbishops, bishops, doctors of law and medicine sat arrayed opposite the chair to which Joan was led. The battle lines were drawn. On one side the shrewdest intellects of the time, backed by English power and English money; on the other, an illiterate girl of nineteen, alone.

The trial was a total sham, as it was held under the auspices of Bishop Cauchon, who had no jurisdiction and was a puppet cleric who held his office at the pleasure of the English government. The outcome was a foregone conclusion. Further, it broke all the ecclesiastical law as no defense counsel was provided for Joan. The clerical notary, Nicholas Bailly, commissioned to collect testimony against Joan, could find no adverse evidence, without which the court had no grounds to even initiate a trial.

Bishop Cauchon called for the holy book of Evangel for Joan to take the oath to tell the truth. Joan refused to take the oath declaring, "I cannot take the oath, as I do not know what you will question me about. You may ask me things that I must not tell you."

Pierre Cauchon turned as purple as his robe; the examiners murmured. Never before had such a thing happened.

"You are asked only to tell truth about matters of religion and other things that you know."

"I will willingly swear concerning my father and mother and whatever I've done since coming into France. As for my revelations from God, I've never disclosed them to anyone but Charles, my king, and I am not going to reveal them here, either—not even if you cut off my head…Eight days from now I'll know whether I can tell you about them," she added, playing for time.

The bishop had no choice but to administer the oath on Joan's terms. Routine questions and answers followed until Cauchon asked her to recite the Lord's Prayer, which Joan said she would willingly do if allowed to offer her confession. Confession was not forthcoming, of course, nor was she allowed to hear the Mass, which she asked for. Much time was spent in verbal jousting. Finally, Cauchon abjured Joan, on pain of being a pronounced heretic, not to attempt to escape from her prison.

"I do accept your command," answered Joan. "If I managed to escape, no one could accuse me of breaking my word, since I've given it to no one. Besides," she exclaimed, "I protest against being kept in chains and irons in my cell."

Day after day, she acquitted herself very eloquently and bested the loaded questions that the prosecution posed her. In one notable exchange, she was asked if she was in God's grace, a scholarly trap. By church doctrine, no one can say if they are in God's grace or not. A "yes" answer would have condemned her for heresy. A "no" answer would have been construed as a confession of guilt. Her answer was both brilliant and classic; "*If I am not, may God put me there, and if I am, may God so keep me.*

At her trial Joan said that she feared "no woman in Rouen in sewing and spinning," thus attesting to her feminine virtues. Trying to trick her at her trial, she was asked whether St. Michael wore his hair long or carried a balance. Joan refused to answer but declared, "I see the voices through the eyes of my body as well as I see you."

Bishop Cauchon denied Joan's appeals to the Council of Basel and the Pope.

This glorious young woman was burned at the stake in the market place in Rouen on May 30, 1431. She was nineteen years old. Her last word was *Jesus*.

Historical note: Pope Callixtus III authorized a "nullification trial." In July 1456, she was declared innocent and a martyr. Bishop Cauchon was indicted for heresy.

Joan was beatified in 1909 and canonized on the sixteenth of May, 1920.

And there is an upside, as you can go to Rouen's market place and stand alongside the exact spot where the stake was set and let your tears flow. Then go into Joan's church which is adjacent, kneel, and allow her undying spirit to flow into you. You will arise a much better person. I did.

Sources: Churchill: History of the
English Speaking People

The Saint and the Devil

ELIZABETH TUDOR: THE VIRGIN QUEEN

Now you are thinking, *How could this woman be an inspiration? After all, she was princess born with a silver spoon in her mouth—she must have had it made.* Nothing could be further from the truth. And don't allow yourself to be misguided by paintings of her. The portrait painters of that era would probably have been better employed at painting houses rather than ladies. If the women actually resembled their pictures, the human race would probably have become extinct a long time ago.

She was known as the Virgin Queen, and English schoolboys liked to add, "and as a queen, she was a great success." Be that as it may, she turned out to be an excellent monarch and probably the best England ever had. Her father was Henry VIII, and her mother, Anne Boleyn. Henry did have some good qualities, and Elizabeth inherited most of them; she was charismatic. She had a commanding carriage and a natural dignity, high courage in moments of crisis, a fiery and imperious resolution when defied, and an almost inexhaustible amount of physical energy. She excelled at sports.

Queen Elizabeth I reigned from September 1533 until March 1603 and was the fifth and last monarch of the Tudor dynasty. Her childhood and adolescence were traumatic to put it mildly and fraught with danger. With the execution of her mother when she was two-and-a-half years old, she was declared illegitimate and banished from the court. She was placed in the care of a succession of lady mistresses who were responsible for the young girl's education, and most of them did an outstanding job. Elizabeth was a willing student, and by the time her formal education was concluded in 1550, she was the best educated woman of her generation and spoke six languages. Elizabeth lived by her motto—*Video et taceo* ("I see and say nothing").

Succeeding Henry VIII was Edward VI, the son of Jane Seymour. He reigned through a Regency as he never reached maturity. He reinforced the Protestant faith in England and abolished celibacy, the Mass, and ordered that church services be conducted in English. He bequeathed the crown to Lady Jane Grey, the daughter of Mary Tudor, queen of France, and great niece of Henry VIII, thus cutting his sisters out of the succession. Jane had the shortest reign in history, and she spent it entirely in the Tower of London.

Upon Henry's passing, his last wife, Catherine Parr, married Thomas Seymour, brother of the lord protector, the duke of Somerset. Catherine and Thomas took the fourteen-year-old Elizabeth into their household in Chelsea. Elizabeth was almost certainly sexually molested by Seymour, which may have affected her for the rest of her life. Catherine caught the two of them in an embrace, and Elizabeth was sent away.

Mary I, who succeeded her brother, was the eldest surviving daughter of Henry VIII and Catherine of Aragon. Mary married King Philip II of Spain, which made her extremely unpopular with the population of England. Her intention was to restore Catholicism in England. During her five-year reign, she had three hundred religious dissenters burned at the stake, hence her sobriquet "Bloody Mary." (In the last thirty years of Elizabeth's reign, she executed about the same number of Catholics for treason.) Mary even went as far to have a terrified Elizabeth imprisoned in the Tower of London, for nearly a year, on suspicion of collaboration with Protestant activists. Any false step or slip of the tongue, and it would have been "off with her head." When it appeared that Mary was pregnant, Elizabeth was no longer considered a threat, and she was allowed to return to her home at Hatfield under house arrest.

After Catherine Parr died, Thomas renewed his attentions to Elizabeth, hoping to marry her. He was arrested on suspicion of plotting to overthrow the king and marry Elizabeth. Under questioning, his past conduct came to light, and he was beheaded in 1549. It should be noted that Elizabeth maintained complete silence during the investigation, although her interrogator said, "I do see it in her face that she is guilty."

Elizabeth's comment following his execution was, "Today died a man of much wit and very little judgment."

Upon the death of Mary in November 1558, Elizabeth ascended the throne and inherited a troubled England and a hazardous enterprise—the monarchy. England had only one ally, and that was Catholic Spain. France was hostile, which shouldn't be surprising, given the Hundred Years War, *et al.* England's last toehold in France—Calais—was gone. The Franco-Scottish alliance threatened to the north, and Mary, queen of Scots, the wife of the French Dauphin, actually had a better claim to the throne than Elizabeth. The situation at the treasury was desperate, and English credit was poor, with the money markets of Europe charging 14 percent interest on loans to Britain. Catholics and Protestants were at each other's throats.

A former clerk of the Council to Edward VI put it succinctly:

> The queen poor, the realm exhausted, the nobility poor and decayed. Want of good captains and soldiers, the people out of order. Justice not executed. All things dear (*expensive*). Excess in meat, drink and apparel. Divisions among ourselves. The French King bestriding the realm, having one foot in Calais and the other in Scotland. Steadfast enmity but no steadfast friendship abroad.

Not a pretty picture for a young queen.

Wisely, she immediately surrounded herself with men of astute mind, with whom she met daily; Matthew Parker, a future archbishop of Canterbury; Nicholas Bacon whom she appointed lord keeper of the Great Seal; Robert Ascham, the foremost scholar of the day; and most notable of all, William Cecil, Baron Burghley, who served her faithfully for most of her reign, until his death in 1598. He was twice secretary of state and lord high treasurer from 1572. Elizabeth charged Cecil thus:

"This judgment I have of you, that you will not be corrupted by any manner of gifts, that you will be faithful to the State, and that, without respect to any private will, you will give me that counsel that you think best."

Her first order of business was to strive for religious peace at home and achieve safety from Scotland. She repealed Mary's Catholic legislation and made England Protestant by law. She declared herself supreme governor of the English church, later to be known as the Church of England. But running deep among some disenchanted minds was the notion that a man should be free to worship his God in his own way and not be bound by doctrines or rigorous rules and regulations imposed by Rome or Canterbury. This idea was about as alien to the mind set of most people of the day as being able to choose which laws to obey or which judge to choose.

Enter the Puritans who had fled Bloody Mary's reign of terror and were now to have a great role in English history. Puritanism was democratic in theory and organization but totally intolerant in practice.

French troops supported the French queen-mother in Scotland, but there was an active Puritan group that opposed them. Elizabeth had the fleet blockade the Scottish ports to interdict reinforcements. Then John Knox, in exile in Geneva, raised his voice against foreign rule and he was allowed to re-enter Scotland by way of England. He also denounced "the monstrous regiment of women." He didn't like the idea of countries being ruled by women. His preaching in Scotland had a profound impact, and Elizabeth sent a small military force on behalf of the Scottish Protestants, which prevailed, and by the Treaty of Leith, the Protestant cause was assured in Scotland forever.

All this time Parliament was urging the queen to marry so that there would be no doubt of succession to the throne. She was not without suitors, but her wise mind realized that whomsoever she married, there would sure to be political consequences or even international repercussions. She also had her memories of the Seymour incident and her father's disastrous marriages. She did have a deep and lasting affection for Robert Dudley, younger son of the earl of Northumberland, whom she made the earl of Leicester. But Elizabeth's main loyalty was to her people, and she wanted to keep them safe from civil war or foreign intervention. She just said, "No."

The return of Mary, queen of Scots, to her homeland was cause for concern. Interestingly, Mary's mother-in-law, Catherine de Medicis, became regent over Charles IX, so that three countries—England, France, and Scotland—were ruled by women at the same time. But of the three, only Elizabeth kept her grip.

At this time, the north of England was largely Catholic, and some of the nobles would have liked to have Mary's hand in marriage. Elizabeth knew her rival and knew that Mary was incapable of separating her emotions from her politics. Mary lacked the vigilant self-control that Elizabeth had learned from the bitter years of her childhood.

Mary had entered into several bad marriages, even marrying the murderer of one of her husbands. After strife and imprisonment in Scotland, she threw herself upon the mercy of the waiting Elizabeth.

Mary in England proved to be more dangerous than Mary in Scotland. The earls of Northumberland and Westmoreland staged a pro-Catholic uprising in the North, but before they could seize Mary, the queen had her conveyed South in the custody of her cousin on the Boleyn side, Lord Hunsdon. The Northern lords were hoping that the Southern Catholic lords would join forces with them, but when that did not happen, the rebels broke into small parties, many of them scurrying across the border into Scotland.

Pope Pius V, a former inquisitor general, excommunicated Elizabeth, thus providing Spain with spiritual ammunition should the need for attacking England arise. Next Rome sent missionaries of a most formidable type—Jesuits. A totally dedicated group which held their lives as unimportant compared to their mission of restoring England to Rome's fold and were prepared to die for their efforts.

Cecil's deputy, Francis Walsingham, established a very effective secret service and flushed out many of the Jesuit cells, deploying agents to infiltrate them. Those which escaped his dragnet fled to Scotland. Some Tudor houses in England have "priest holes" where the Jesuit missionaries hid while Walsingham's agents conducted their searches.

Events were now moving quickly toward armed conflict with Spain. Dutch Protestants had been resisting Spanish occupation for years, and in midsummer 1584, a leader of the revolt, William the Silent, was fatally wounded at his home in Delft by a Spanish agent. Elizabeth sent Lord Leicester with an expeditionary force to shore up Dutch resistance in the Netherlands. English anti-Spanish opinion flared and focused on Mary, whose connivance in plots against Elizabeth's life was now coming to light. The queen saw that Mary's death was a political necessity. She was tried, found guilty, and Elizabeth reluctantly signed Mary's death warrant. Without going into details, suffice it to say that she went to her death with dignity and courage. The English people rejoiced, but Spain prepared for the invasion of England.

English seamen, notably Francis Drake and John Hawkins, had been raiding ports in Spain's colonies in South and Central America and plundering Spanish treasure galleons as they sailed home from their American possessions. Drake, who the Spanish referred as the "Master Thief of the Unknown World," had raided Cadiz in Spain and destroyed a huge amount of war materiel, which set Philip's plans back by a year, all with Elizabeth's full knowledge.

John Hawkins had been appointed controller of the navy and had rebuilt the Royal Navy that Henry VIII founded. He was turning out warships that he felt sure could stand up to any the Spaniards could send against them. He armed them with long range heavy cannon—culverins, so that they could stand off, out of range of the Spanish guns and shoot them up.

The queen's sailors had also been busy exploring America's eastern seaboard. They took possession of Newfoundland. In 1585 the English established a small colony on Roanoke Island and christened it Virginia in Elizabeth's honor. The land area comprised approximately modern day Virginia and North Carolina.

The Spanish plan for invasion was to sail up the English Channel with an enormous Armada and fight their way, if necessary, to Gravelines and embark a corps of 16,000 veterans from the duke of Parma's army in the Netherlands and land in the Thames Estuary in Essex. The Armada already had over 20,000 soldiers of dubious quality on board. The Spanish fleet comprised one hundred and thirty ships mounting 2500 guns. Twenty were galleons; forty-four were armed merchant ships; eight were galleys, and the rest were unarmed transports. The queen's ships numbered thirty-four, but the fleet was augmented by private vessels pressed into service, but most of them were too small to be of assistance to Hawkins and his captains.

The English plan was to intercept the Armada in the western approaches and have a squadron stationed at the eastern end of the Channel and endeavor to prevent the Spanish linkup. Meanwhile, an army of 20,000, led by the queen herself, with Lord Leicester, would march down to the Tilbury area of Essex and await the invading army from Spain. Wearing a silver breastplate over a white velvet dress, she addressed her troops:

> My loving people, we have been persuaded by some that are careful of our safety, to take heed how we commit ourself to armed multitudes for fear of treachery, but I assure you, I do not desire to live to distrust my faithful and loving people…I know I have but the body of a weak and feeble woman, but I have the heart and stomach of a king, and of a king of England too, and think foul scorn that Parma or Spain, or any Prince of Europe should dare to invade the borders of my realm.
>
> Encyclopedia Britannica

The invasion never came—the queen's sailors had seen to that. The Armada had a very rough passage from Tagus to the English Channel via Corunna. It arrived off the coast of Cornwall on July 12. The English fleet put to sea, under the flag of Howard of Effingham, and found themselves in a precarious situation to leeward of the Spanish. If Admiral Medina-Sidonia had attacked the English at that point, he might have met with some success, but his orders were to embark Parma's troops, so he just stood up the Channel toward Gravelines. That missed opportunity may have cost him the battle, as it gave Howard the opportunity to take the weather gauge. The quick little English ships harried the Spanish for nine days with great success. Now Medina-Sidonia made a fatal mistake: he anchored his fleet off Calais. Howard was joined by the rest of his ships, which had been guarding the eastern end of the Channel, and he resolved to attack after dark. Eight of the vessels from the eastern squadron were filled with explosives, set on fire and allowed to drift down into the anchored Armada. When the Spanish captains woke up to their danger, they cut their cables and tried to get back out to sea. Dozens of collisions ensued, and the *San Lorenzo* lost her rudder and ran aground in Calais harbor. Medina and the rest of the fleet, aided by a SSW wind, proceeded to Gravelines only to discover that Parma's troops were not waiting for him. The Spaniards now turned to face their attackers, and a savage close quarter's battle raged for eight hours, during which Howard destroyed eight Spanish vessels, but the English fleet was now out of ammunition.

The Spanish fleet sailed round the North of Scotland and down the western coast of Ireland and lost seventeen more ships owing to the gales, which they encountered once back in the Atlantic. The English did not lose a single ship. England was now firmly established as a World power.

Shakespeare wrote in *King John:*

"Come the three corners of the world in arms,

And we shall shock them. Naught shall make us rue

If England to itself do rest but true."

William Shakespeare

Queen Elizabeth's long reign is regarded as a golden age. The arts flourished with playwrights like William Shakespeare and Christopher Marlowe. She loved her subjects and they her, and they dubbed her "Good Queen Bess." Although she was an "absolute monarch," she did listen to her councilors and advisers, for which some historians fault her.

When she died in the early hours of the morning of March 24, 1603, England was the most powerful country in Europe.

Sources: Churchill: History of the
English Speaking People

HARRIET TUBMAN: ABOLITIONIST, SUFFRAGIST, SPY, WAR HERO

THREE HUNDRED DOLLARS REWARD

RAN AWAY from the subscriber on Monday On the 17 ult., three negroes, named as follows: **HARRY** aged about 19 years, has on one side of his neck a wen just under the ear, he is of dark chestnut color, about 5 feet 8 or 9 inches hight; **BEN** aged about 25 years, is very quick to speak when spoken to, he is of chestnut color, about six feet high; **MINTY**, aged about 27 years, is of a chestnut color, fine looking, and about 5 feet high. One hundred dollars reward will be given for each of the above named negroes if taken out of the State, and $50 each if taken in the State. They must be lodged in Baltimore, Easton or Cambridge Jail, in Maryland.

ELIZA ANN BRODESS

Near Bucktown, Dorchester county,
Md. Oct. 3d , 1849.
The Delaware Gazette will please copy the above three weeks, and charge this office.

Runaway Notice published in the Cambridge *Democrat*

Born Araminta Ross, circa 1820 or 1821, died March 10, 1913. She was born to slave parents, Harriet "Rit" Green and Ben Ross. She is the epitome of courage and determination.

At the age of six, she was hired out to a woman called "Miss Susan" as a nursemaid, and her job was to watch a baby while it slept. When the baby awoke, it cried, so Minty was whipped for that. One day she was whipped five times before breakfast and bore the scars for the rest of her life, not to mention the mental scars. On another day she was accused of stealing a cube of sugar, and in an attempt to avoid punishment, she hid in a pigsty for five days and competed with the pigs for scraps of food.

Starving, she returned to Miss Susan's house and received a severe beating. In order to protect herself from the pain of whippings and beatings, she wrapped herself up in layers of clothing and exaggerated her cries whenever she was beaten or whipped. On one occasion she bit a white man's knee during punishment. The man apparently kept his distance from her after that.

She was hired out to various plantation owners, one of whom was named James Cook. Cook required her to go into the river and check on the muskrat traps and, even when suffering from measles, was made to continue with her tasks. When she became very ill, she was sent back to her mother, who nursed her back to health. As she grew older and stronger, she was assigned to field work, hauling logs, or driving cattle.

As an adolescent she was sent on an errand to a store. Inside the store was a young man who was AWOL from his employment. The man's overseer caught up with him and demanded that Minty help to restrain the young man. Minty refused, and the truant ran out of the store. The enraged overseer picked up a two pound weight to hurl at the runaway, missed, and struck Minty in the head instead. Bleeding and unconscious, she was returned to her owner's house and was laid on a bench for two days without attention of any kind. She later considered that her unkempt hair "which stood up like a bushel" saved her life.

About this time she became deeply religious and remembered the Bible stories that her mother had taught her. She rejected any notion that the scriptures alluded to anything about slaves being obedient. She found guidance in the stories in the Old Testament about deliverance, and some of those are in this book. The head wound caused her to have "visions" from time to time and potent dreams. She considered these to be guidance from God.

In 1840, Minty's father Ben was manumitted, meaning he was freed from slavery by a former owner's will, which stipulated that Ben would be free at the age of forty-five. Of course many owners overlooked such stipulations if the slave was still valuable as a worker. In Ben's case, he was more like fifty-five when he was freed from bondage. Ross continued to work for the Thompson family as a timber estimator and foreman.

In 1844, Minty married a free black man named John Tubman and became Harriet Tubman. Under the odious culture of slavery in the United States at that time, as Harriet was still a slave, any children of she and her husband would be automatically enslaved. Many years later, Harriet hired a lawyer to look into her mother, Rit's, status. It was discovered that a former owner had issued instructions that Rit was to be manumitted at age forty-five. But the Pattison and Brodess families cheerfully ignored this stipulation, and Harriet realized that it would be an impossible task to see it enacted.

In 1849, Tubman became ill again, which diminished her value as a slave, and Edward Brodess unsuccessfully tried to sell her. Angered by this, Harriett prayed to God for Brodess to change his ways. When it appeared that her sale was imminent, she switched tactics and began praying for the demise of Mr. Brodess. A week later her prayer was answered, and he dropped dead.

This brings up an interesting point, as I have been suggesting to you that thought forces should only be deployed with positive thoughts in mind, and Harriet's certainly were not. A possible explanation is that her heart was so pure that the prayer for her master's health worked rather well, but in the second instance that her when so powerfully focused and completely negatively on Brodess that they doomed him.

Brodess' widow, Eliza, began actively working to sell her family's slaves, and Tubman decided not to wait for someone else to decide her fate, and over her husband's objections, she and her two brothers, Ben and Henry, made a break for it on the seventeenth of September, 1849. She later said, "There was one of two things that I had a right to: liberty or death; if I could not have one, I would have the other."

Harriet's brothers became weak at the knees and returned to their owner, forcing their sister to return with them. It did not take long for Tubman to escape again, this time alone. She sent a coded message to her mother via a trusted slave named Mary. It was a song which ran, "I'll meet you in the morning; I'm bound for the promised land."

She certainly used the Underground Railroad, which was a network of secret routes and safe houses with routes to Canada and Mexico. Escaping slaves were assisted by abolitionists and the Society of Friends, the Quakers. It is estimated that over 100,000 slaves escaped this way.

Her dangerous journey made it necessary to travel by night, and she guided herself by the Pole star. She had to avoid the vigilant eyes of slave catchers. At one her earliest stops on the Railroad, the lady of the house ordered her to sweep the yard, making it appear that Tubman worked for the family. After nightfall, her hosts hid her in a cart and took her to the next friendly "station."

When she finally crossed into Pennsylvania, she did so with feelings of relief and awe.

"When I found that I had crossed the line, I looked at my hands to see if to see if I was the same person. There was such a glory over everything; the sun came like gold through the trees, and over the fields, and I felt like I was in heaven."

After reaching Philadelphia, the city of brotherly (and sisterly) love, the kindly US Congress passed the Fugitive Slave Law of 1850, which compelled law enforcement officials to aid in the capture of runaway slaves, even in states which had outlawed slavery. Meanwhile, racial tension was increasing in Philadelphia itself.

In December 1850, Harriet learned that her niece, Kassiah, was to be sold, along with her two children, in Cambridge, Maryland. Tubman went to Baltimore where her brother-in-law, Tom Tubman, hid her until the time of the sale. Kassiah's husband, John Bowley, a free black man, made the winning bid for his wife. Then, while Bowley pretended to arrange the payment on the sale, Kassiah and the children were taken to a safe house. When night fell Bowley ferried his family by canoe sixty miles to Baltimore, where they met up with Tubman, who brought them all to safety in Philadelphia.

Harriet worked closely with Thomas Garrett, a Quaker, who had an iron and hardware business in Wilmington, Delaware. . He worked openly as Station Master on the last stop of the Underground Railroad in the state. The authorities were well aware of his activities, but he was never arrested. He and a fellow Quaker, John Hunn were tried and found guilty of helping a family of slaves to escape in 1848. Both men were fined, but a compromised settlement was reached and Garrett's house was liened. With the aid of friends, he was able to pay off the lien and continued running his hardware business and helping runaways to gain their freedom.

In the spring of 1851, Tubman went back to Maryland and brought out her brother Moses and two other men. Word of her exploits encouraged her family, and she became more confident with each trip to Maryland, and as she led more and more slaves to freedom she became known as "Moses," an allusion to the Hebrew icon from the Old Testament.

In the fall of 1851, Tubman went back to Dorchester County, this time to find her husband, John. She saved up some money and bought him a suit, only to find that he had married another woman named Caroline. Harriet sent word that John should join her, but he insisted that he was happy where he was. Tubman considered going to his house and making a scene but finally decided that he wasn't worth the effort. Instead she found some slaves who wanted to escape and led them to Philadelphia.

Thanks to the Fugitive Slave Law, the northern United States was very dangerous for runaways, and they tended to migrate into Canada. In December 1851, Harriet guided a group of eleven fugitives northward. Evidence suggests that the group stayed at the home of former slave Frederick Douglass. It was a difficult time for Douglass to find the money to get them on their way to Canada and providing food while they were under his roof.

Douglass and Tubman enjoyed mutual admiration as they worked together against slavery in the United States. When an early biography of Harriet was being prepared, Frederick Douglass wrote a letter to honor her:

> You ask for what you do not need when you call upon me for a word of commendation. I need such words from you far more than you can need them from me, especially where your superior labors and devotion to the cause of the lately enslaved of our land as I know them. The difference between us is

very marked. Most that I have done and suffered in the service of our cause has been in public, and I have received much encouragement every step of the way. You on the other hand, have labored in a private way. I have wrought in the day—you in the night…The midnight sky and the silent stars have been the witnesses of your devotion to freedom and of your heroism. Excepting John Brown—of sacred memory—I know of no one who has willingly encountered more perils and hardships to serve our enslaved people than you have.

The Moses of her People. Sarah H. Bradford

Harriet Tubman kept up this activity for eleven years traveling again and again to Maryland, rescuing some seventy slaves and her three brothers, Henry, Ben, and Robert. She also provided specific information and instructions to sixty other fugitives to escape to the north. Her adventures involved enormous personal risk, and she used many different disguises and subterfuges to avoid detection.

Once, she wore a bonnet and carried two live chickens, as though she was running errands, and suddenly finding herself walking toward a former owner, she pulled on the string securing the birds' legs. They made such a commotion that she was able to avoid eye contact. On another occasion she recognized a fellow passenger on a train as a former master. She snatched a newspaper and pretended to read it. As she was known to be illiterate, the man ignored her.

Harriet acquired faith at the time of her injury. She spoke of "consulting with God." Her faith in God always provided immediate assistance, much as Joan of Arc's voices did. It's an interesting coincidence that both great heroines were illiterate. Tubman also carried a revolver, and if her escapees showed any inclination to turn back, Tubman threatened to shoot them, with the words, "You go on or die."

One of her last missions was to rescue her parents. Her father, Ben, had purchased Rit for twenty dollars from Eliza Brodess in 1855. Even though they were both free, the area was very hostile to them, and two years later, Harriet received word that her father was in danger of arrest for harboring a group of eight escapees. Harriet traveled once more to Maryland and took them to St. Catherine's Ontario in Canada.

Years later she told an audience that, "I was conductor of the Underground Railroad for eight years, and I can say what most conductors can't say—I never ran my train off the track, and I never lost a passenger."

The year was 1858, and in April she was introduced to John Brown, an abolitionist who advocated violence to destroy slavery in the United States. Tubman never thought of using violence against white people but agreed nevertheless with his course of direct action and his goals. Brown spoke of being called by God and trusted to the divine to protect him from the wrath of the slaveholders

As Brown began recruiting supporters for an attack on slaveholders, he was joined by "General" Tubman as he called her. Tubman's knowledge of resources and support networks was invaluable to Brown and his planners. Other notable abolitionists like Frederick Douglass and William Lloyd Garrison did not endorse his tactics. Brown dreamed of fighting to create a new state for freed slaves, and accordingly made plans for military action. He thought that when the battle was joined that slaves would rise up and carry out a rebellion across the south. He asked Tubman to gather former slaves then living in Canada who would be willing to join his fighting force. Harriet did that.

On May 8, 1858, John Brown held a meeting in Chatham-Kent, Ontario, where he unveiled his plan for the raid on Harper's Ferry, Virginia. Word, however, was leaked to the authorities, and Brown delayed the attack and continued to raise funds. Tubman assisted in this effort and made more detailed plans for the assault.

Harriet was very busy at this time, tending to her family, and giving talks to abolitionist groups. Brown was unable to contact Tubman, and when the raid took place, she was not present. Many reasons have been advanced for her absence ranging from sickness, through rescuing more slaves, to doubts on the viability of the plan. The last is probably the most likely reason. Remember, she did not espouse violence.

The raid ended in failure, and Brown was hanged for treason. He was viewed as a noble martyr, and "his soul goes marching on."

The *Dred Scott* decision of 1857, in which the noble United States Supreme Court ruled seven to two that people of African descent, imported into the United States as slaves, or their descendants, had no rights under the Constitution and could never become citizens, etc. ad nauseam. This must have enraged Tubman and the abolitionists. The Fourteenth Amendment of 1868 went a long way toward overruling that unjust Supreme Court decision.

In early 1859, abolitionist US Senator William H. Seward sold Tubman a small parcel of land near Auburn, NY, which became a haven for Harriet's family and friends. She took in boarders and offered a safe place for African Americans seeking a better life in the north.

November 1860 saw Harriet Tubman's last rescue mission. She went back to Dorchester County. During the 1850s, she had been unable to rescue her sister, Rachel, and her two children, Ben and Angenine. She discovered that Rachel had died and that the children could only be rescued for a thirty dollar bribe. Never one to waste a trip, Tubman gathered another group, including the Ennals family. It was a particularly difficult mission, as the slave catchers were very active, and the weather was unseasonably cold. They had little food. They had to hide out for long periods and drug the little ones to keep them quiet. They reached safety on December 28th, 1860.

When the American Civil War started, Tubman had high hopes for a Union victory, which would be a key step toward the abolition of slavery. General Ben Butler was already aiding escaped slaves flooding into Fort Monroe. He declared them to be contraband and properly seized by the US Army—he put them to work, without pay, in the fort. Tubman was anxious to join forces with the army and joined a group of abolitionists from Boston and Philadelphia and headed for Hilton Head in South Carolina. Harriet became a familiar figure in the camps, especially in Port Royal.

Tubman soon met General David Hunter, a strong supporter of abolition. General Hunter declared all his contrabands free and began forming a regiment of black soldiers. President Lincoln was not yet prepared to enforce emancipation in the southern states and reprimanded Hunter for his actions.

Harriet condemned Lincoln for his general unwillingness to consider ending slavery in the United States. "God won't let master Lincoln beat the South till he does the right thing," she said.

> *"Master Lincoln, he's a great man, and I am a poor negro; but the negro can tell master Lincoln how to save money and the young men. He can do it by setting the negro free. Suppose that there was an awful big snake down there, on the floor. He bite you. Folks all scared, because you die. You send for a doctor to cut the bite, but the snake, he all rolled up there, and while the doctor is doing it, he bite you again. The doctor dug out that bite; but while the doctor is doing it, the snake, he spring up and bite you again; so he keep doing it, till you kill* him. *That's what master Lincoln ought to know."*

Lydia Maria Child (1862) by Columbia University

Harriet served as a nurse in Port Royal, making remedies from the local plants and treating soldiers with dysentery and aiding those with smallpox.

Lincoln finally put the Proclamation of Emancipation into effect in January 1863. Tubman considered it a giant step toward liberating black people from slavery. Before long she was leading a band of scouts through the land around Port Royal. The terrain was similar to that of the eastern shore of Maryland, and her knowledge of covert travel and subterfuge among enemies was put to good use. Tubman's group, under orders from secretary of war, Edwin M. Stanton, mapped the unfamiliar terrain and reconnoitered the inhabitants. Later she worked alongside Colonel James Montgomery and provided him with key intelligence which aided the capture of Jacksonville, Florida.

Later that year Harriet Tubman became the first woman to lead an armed assault during the Civil War, when Montgomery and his troops conducted an assault on a collection of plantations along the Combahee River. Tubman guided three US Navy ships around Confederate mines. Once ashore, the Union troops set fire to the plantations, destroying the buildings and seizing thousands of dollars' worth of food and supplies. When the ships sounded their whistles and the slaves realized that the area was being liberated, hundreds of men, women, and children rushed toward the ships and clambered aboard. As Confederate troops rushed to the scene, the steamboats, bearing more than seven hundred slaves, took off toward Beaufort. Newspapers heralded Harriet's "patriotism, sagacity, energy, and ability." Most of the newly liberated men joined the Union army.

For two more years, Tubman worked for the Union forces, tending to newly liberated slaves, scouting into Confederate territory, and eventually nursing wounded soldiers in Virginia. She made several trips back to Auburn to care for her parents. The Confederacy surrendered in April 1865, and after giving several more months of service, Tubman headed home.

Despite her years of service, she had never received a regular salary and was, for years, denied compensation. As usual, the US government was slow in recognizing its debt to her, and she did not receive a pension for her service in the Civil War until 1899.

Harriet Tubman returned home at the end of the war. During a train ride to New York, the conductor told her to move into the smoking car. She refused, explaining her government service. The conductor cursed her and grabbed her, but she resisted, and he summoned two other passengers for help. While she clutched at the railing, this gallant trio muscled her away, breaking her arm in the process. They threw her into the smoking car, causing more injuries.

Harriet Tubman spent her remaining years looking after her family and others in need and took in boarders to help pay the bills. One of her boarders was a Civil War veteran named Nelson Davis, and they soon fell in love, although he was twenty-two years younger than she. They spent the next twenty years together and in 1874 adopted a baby girl named Gertie.

She suffered poverty, and friends and admirers raised funds to support her. Sarah H. Bradford wrote an authorized biography entitled *Scenes in the Life of Harriet Tubman*. The book raised $1,200 for Tubman. Bradford published another book called *Harriet, the Moses of her People* as a way to further alleviate Tubman's poverty.

A very unsavory incident befell her in 1873, when two con men, Messrs. Stevenson and Thomas, told Harriet that they had smuggled a cache of gold out of the South worth about $5,000 and that she could have it for $2,000. Poor honest, trusting Harriet fell for the con and even took the villains into her home for several days. She borrowed the money from a wealthy friend named Anthony Shimer and arranged to receive the gold late at night. The thugs lured her into the woods, attacked her, and knocked her out with chloroform, bound and gagged her, then stole her purse. New York responded to the incident with outrage, and while some criticized her for being so naïve, most sympathized with her and remembered her service to her country and reduced her circumstances. Wisconsin Representative Gerry W. Hazleton introduced a bill (H. R. 3786) providing that Tubman be paid "the sum of $2,000 for services rendered by her to the Union Army as scout, nurse and spy…" The Congress defeated the bill.

Harriet now turned her attention to the cause of women's suffrage and was soon working alongside Susan B. Anthony and Emily Howland. She traveled and spoke at meetings in New York, Boston, and Washington, D.C. She used the sacrifices of countless women throughout modern history as evidence of women's equality to men. Once asked if she believed that women should have the suffrage, she responded, "I suffered enough to believe it." When the National Federation of Afro-American Women was founded in 1896, she was the keynote speaker at its first meeting.

Worn out from work and injuries, Harriet Tubman died of pneumonia on March 10, 1913. She was buried with full military honors at Fort Hill Cemetery in Auburn. The city commemorated her life with a plaque on the courthouse. The wording on the plaque is written in the vernacular, but it is meant to say, "I never ran my train off the track."

MARY SEACOLE:
THE ANGEL FROM JAMAICA

See, here is Mary Seacole, who did as much in the Crimea as another magic-lamping lady, but being dark; could scarce be seen for the flame of Florence's candle.

Salman Rushdie, *The Satanic Verses*

Mary Seacole was born to Scottish officer of the British army and a Jamaican woman who was a "doctress." Mary's mother ran a boarding house called Blundell Hall and a good hotel in Kingston, Jamaica. Many of her residents were disabled European soldiers and sailors, who she treated with traditional West Indian and African herbal remedies. Many were suffering from yellow fever, which was endemic in the area in the early nineteenth century. The sickness was transmitted by mosquitoes, which are abundant in Central America and Africa. It causes, among other unpleasant symptoms, jaundice, hence the name. Today we have safe and effective vaccine to prevent the onset of yellow fever.

In the late eighteenth century and early nineteenth, a third of Britain's foreign trade was with the West

Indies, and her economic interests were protected by an extremely large military presence.

Mary acquired her nursing skills from her mother, of course, who had her practice on dolls, then pets, and finally being allowed to assist her mother in the treatment of patients.

Seacole proudly referred to herself as a Creole, which is not a racial slur but was used to define her as a child of a white settler. She was also proud of her relationship with black African slaves, brought there by the British. She spent a number of years in the household of an elderly woman of means, where she was treated as a member of the family and received an excellent education. Later on as an educated daughter of a British officer, and a free black woman with a respectable business, Mary enjoyed a high position in Jamaican society.

Mary went to London in 1821 and stayed with relatives for a year before returning to Jamaica. Seacole returned to London a year later with a large stock of West Indian pickles and preserves for sale. It is unknown whether or not she was successful as a vendor in London.

Returning to Jamaica in 1825, she nursed her old patroness through an illness until she died a few years later. Seacole moved back into Blundell Hall and worked alongside her mother. She was occasionally called to the military hospital at Up-Park Camp, the HQ of the British army.

In 1836, Mary married Edwin Horatio Hamilton Seacole, a merchant with poor health. The couple opened a provisions store in Black River, a thriving seaport, in the sugar, logwood, hides, peppers, and rum trades. Nowadays it is a tourist center and the gateway to Treasure Beach resort area. The venture was a failure, and they returned to Blundell Hall after four years.

Edwin's middle names are rather interesting and bear further examination. According to Seacole family legend, Edwin was the illegitimate son of Admiral Lord *Horatio* Nelson and his mistress, Lady Emma *Hamilton*. Edwin was adopted by one Thomas, a surgeon, apothecary, and male midwife. Mary, in her will, bequeathed a diamond ring to her friend Lord Rokeby, "given to my late husband by his godfather, Admiral Nelson." There is no mention in Nelson's will of this godson. Son or godson, there does appear to be at least a tenuous connection to the famous couple.

In 1843, Mary and her family lost most of their boarding house to fire, and Blundell Hall burned down but was replaced by the New Blundell Hall. Then Edwin died in October 1844, which was a heavy blow to Mary. She grieved in seclusion for several days but bounced back and "turned a bold front to fortune, blunting the edge of her grief sooner than Europeans who nurse their woe secretly in their hearts." She attributed her rapid recovery to her hot Creole blood.

She absorbed herself with work, declining several offers of marriage. She became widely known and respected among the military visitors to Jamaica who often stayed at Blundell Hall. She treated patients in the cholera epidemic of 1850, which killed 32,000 Jamaicans. Seacole believed that the outbreak was brought to the island by a steamship form New Orleans.

In 1850, her half-brother moved to Cruces, Panama, which was on the Isthmus of Panama and forty-five miles up the Chagres River. Then it was on the popular route between the coasts for prospectors to follow the Gold Rush of 1849. The hopeful forty-niners came by boat as far as Cruces, which was at the limit of navigability of the Chagres River, then rode donkeys for twenty miles to the Pacific Ocean. Now we have the Panama Canal, an all-water route. He established the Independence Hotel in the family tradition.

After a year, Seacole came to visit her brother. Soon after, the town was struck by cholera, and she was on hand to treat the first victim, who survived, establishing a reputation for her. The number of patients became a torrent as the disease spread. The wealthy paid her fees, and the poor she treated for free. She did not use opium but rather mustard rubs, poultices, laxatives, lead II acetate, and re-hydrated using water boiled with cinnamon. Her medications had moderate success, and she had but little competition—a timid dentist sent out by the Panamanian government.

As the disease raged through the population, Seacole raged that people gave into the disease too easily and "bowed down before the plague in slavish despair." She herself became infected toward the end of the epidemic but survived.

Despite the problems with disease, Seacole opened the British Hotel, which was more of a restaurant/bar than a hotel. She sometimes had difficulty controlling the rowdy crowd of travelers.

As the rainy season came to an end, Seacole packed up and moved to Gorgona, as did most other traders in Cruces. At a leaving dinner, an American gave a speech in which he said, "God bless the best yaller he ever made. She's so many shades removed from being entirely black. If we could bleach her by any means, we would, and thus make her acceptable in any company she deserves to be."

Seacole was incensed, and in her reply, she said that she would just as happy to have a complexion "as dark as any nigger's" and wished for the general reformation of American manners.

In Gorgona, Mary established a women-only hotel and continued to minister to the sick. She encountered racial prejudice when returning to Jamaica. An American ship refused to take her, and she had to wait to take passage on a British ship. She had not been home long before the Jamaican medical authorities asked her to treat victims of an outbreak of yellow fever in 1853. Seacole organized a nursing service for the hospital at Up-Park Camp composed of Caribbean doctresses who seemed to be immune to the disease.

Mary returned to Panama in 1854 to wind up her business affairs and three months later moved to the New Granada Gold Mining Company at Fort Bowen to provide medical support. New Granada's superintendent, Thomas Day, was a relative of her late husband.

Seacole had read newspaper reports of the outbreak of hostilities against Russia in the Crimea, before she left Jamaica, and news of the escalation of that conflict reached her in Panama, and she determined to go to England and volunteer as a nurse.

The Crimean War lasted from 1854 until 1856. It was fought between Russia and an alliance of England, France, Sardinia, and Turkey (then still part of the Ottoman Empire). It was part of the long-standing contest between European nations to grab the lands of the declining Ottoman Empire. It was notorious for logistical and tactical blunders on both sides. In one instance, a shipment of boots was sent from Britain, but it turned out to consist of only left boots. In another, "The Charge of the Light Brigade," the cavalry assaulted the wrong valley. It was the first "modern war," as it included the use of railways and the telegraph, and it was also documented by photography.

Many thousands of troops from all the counties were drafted to the area, and disease broke out almost immediately. The hospitals were over-crowded, under staffed, and completely unsanitary. The secretary for war, Sidney Herbert, approached Florence Nightingale to form a cadre of nurses and go to the Crimea. She and her nurses left for Turkey on October 21, 1854. Seacole traveled to England carrying letters of recommendation from doctors in Panama and Jamaica. She quickly came up against racial prejudice and got shuffled around. Mary realized that she would not get appointed even if there was a vacancy. Nightingale had exacting standards for her nurses and many volunteers were rejected on the grounds of being too drunk, too old, or just plain lacking in the social graces. Seacole even applied to the Crimean Fund, a charity set up by public subscription, to support the wounded in the Crimea for sponsorship to travel to the Crimea. Once again she was rebuffed.

She decided that she would have to go under her own steam and at her own expense. She had business cards printed and sent them ahead to announce the opening of the British Hotel where there would be "a mess table and comfortable quarters for sick and convalescent officers." Thomas Day arrived, unexpectedly at almost this time. The two decided to form a partnership. They assembled a stock of supplies, and Seacole left for Constantinople aboard the Dutch steamer *Hollander* on its maiden voyage, January 27, 1855. The vessel called at Malta, where Mary met a doctor who had recently left Scutari, in Turkey, and he provided Seacole with a letter of introduction to Florence Nightingale.

Having arrived at the port for Constantinople, Pera, Seacole lost no time crossing the Bosporus in a caique, which is a small sail boat omnipresent in the eastern Mediterranean, to visit Nightingale at the latter's hospital in Scutari. Whilst there, she encountered many of her former patients and friends from the West Indies. Florence declined Mary's offer of help. It certainly could not have been on the grounds of ability, but possibly on considerations of social acceptability

Undaunted, Seacole transferred most of her stores to the transport *Albatross* and the balance to the *Nonpareil* and set out on a four day voyage to the British bridgehead at Balaclava. Lacking proper building materials, she collected driftwood, packing cases, iron sheets, and she salvaged glass and window frames from a village named Kamara. Hiring local labor, she built the British Hotel, which opened in March 1855.

The establishment sold a wide range of merchandise, often on credit, which proved to be a mistake later. Meals were served at the hotel, prepared by a black cook. Outside catering was also available. The hotel was open six days a week but closed on Sundays. It charged for its services, served alcohol. Seacole served early morning coffee to passing travelers before going to the front line to treat casualties. The business prospered despite theft, particularly of livestock.

The straitlaced Florence Nightingale wasn't quite sure what sort of an establishment Mary was running; in letter to her brother-in-law, Sir Henry Verney, she wrote, "She was very kind to the men & what is more, to the officers-& did some good-& made many drunk." She stopped short of referring to it as a brothel—how could she? A lady of her breeding wouldn't know what a brothel was, would she? She also did not realize that front line soldiers need R & R. But to give Nightingale the credit which she richly deserves, when Seacole faced bankruptcy, she contributed generously to the Seacole Testimonial Fund.

Seacole often went out selling provisions near the British camp at Kadikoi and attended to casualties brought out from the trenches. She was widely known to the troops as "Mother Seacole." Once, when attending troops under fire, she dislocated her thumb, which never completely healed. William Russell of *The Times* wrote that Mary was a "warm and successful physician, who doctors and cures all manner of men with extraordinary success. She is always in attendance near the battlefield to aid the wounded and has earned many a poor fellow's blessing."

In August, Seacole was on her way to Cathcart's Hill, a vantage point, to witness the Allies final assault of Sevastopol. The French led the assault, but the British were beaten back. On September 9, the city was ablaze, and the fires were out of control. The city had fallen. The Russians retired to fortifications at the north end of the harbor. Seacole, having obtained a pass, entered the city, thus winning a bet that she would be the first woman to enter Sevastopol after it fell. She toured the city bearing refreshments and visiting the crowded hospital which was full of dead and dying Russians. Her exotic appearance led to her being stopped by French looters. She was rescued by a French officer. She herself "collected" some items from the city, including a church bell, an altar candle, and a ten-foot painting of Mary, the Mother of Jesus.

The war slowed a little after Sevastopol, and Seacole and Thomas Day prospered with soldiers taking the opportunity to relax and enjoy themselves. There were theatrical performances and horse racing for which the British Hotel furnished the catering.

Peace came with the signing of the Treaty of Paris. The troops went home, and Seacole was left with a mountain of unsold provisions with new goods coming daily along with some of her creditors. She auctioned off as much as she could and sold heavily marked down goods to Russians going home,

The evacuation of the Allied armies was completed in July 1856. Seacole was one of the last to leave, arriving back in London almost destitute, and her health was not too good. She considered setting up a shop in Aldershot, Hampshire, with Day, but it never materialized. Aldershot has a large military presence, and you will have noticed her long association with the British army.

She attended a celebration and dinner for 2,000 veterans at the Royal Surrey Gardens. Florence Nightingale was the principal guest of honor, but reports in *The Times* and *The News of the World* indicated that Mary was feted by a huge crowd and had to have "two burly sergeants" to protect her from the crush.

The creditors just kept on coming, of course, and Seacole was forced to move to inexpensive digs in Covent Garden. She was declared bankrupt on November 7, 1856. Thomas Day may have been at the bottom of her financial problems as he dabbled in horse trading and may have set up as an unofficial bank, cashing debts. At her hearing at the bankruptcy court, she wore four military medals—the British Crimea Medal, the French Legion of Honor, the Turkish Order of the Medjidie, and a Sardinian award. Whether or not she was gazetted for these medals, she certainly earned them.

Her financial plight was highlighted in the press; as a consequence a fund was set up to which many prominent people donated money. On January 30, 1857, she and Day were granted certificates discharging them from bankruptcy. Day left for Australia, but Seacole's finances remained low, and she moved to cheaper lodgings in Soho, triggering a plea for subscriptions from *Punch* on May 2.

In the same month, she wanted to go to India to minister to the wounded during the Indian Mutiny. The Seacole Fund Grand Military Festival, a four day event, was held in the Royal Surrey Gardens, and over 1,000 artists performed, including eleven military bands. It was attended by a crowd of about 40,000 and was supported by Major General Lord Rokeby and Lord George Paget. All she netted was fifty-seven pounds sterling. In March 1858, the mutiny was over.

She wrote an autobiographical account of her travels, *Wonderful Adventures of Mrs. Seacole in Many Lands,* dedicated to Major General Lord Rokeby. In the conclusion, she listed the names of the supporters of her fundraising efforts, which included Prince Edward of Saxe-Weimar, the duke of Wellington, duke of Newcastle, Lord Rokeby, William Russell, and other prominent military men. William Howard Russell of the London Times wrote as a preface, "I have witnessed her devotion and her courage...and I trust that England will never forget one who has nursed her sick, who sought out her wounded to aid and succour them and who performed the last offices for some her illustrious dead."

After going back to Jamaica for seven years, she returned to London with the prospect of rendering medical assistance in the Franco-Prussian War. She joined the periphery of the royal circle. Prince Victor of Hohenlohe-Landenburg carved a marble bust of her in 1871, which was exhibited at The Royal Academy in 1872. Prince Victor was a nephew of Queen Victoria and, as a young lieutenant, had been one of Mary's customers at her shop in the Crimea. She became personal masseuse to the princess of Wales who suffered with white leg and rheumatism.

She died of apoplexy at her home in Paddington, London, in 1881. She was buried in St. Mary's Roman Catholic Cemetery, in Kensal Green, London.

Dead and forgotten for a number of years, there has been a resurgence of interest in her in the twenty-first century and efforts to properly acknowledge her achievements. She has become a symbol of racial attitudes and social injustices in Britain during her lifetime.

Mary Seacole was voted into first place in an online poll of 100 *great black Britons* in 2004.

ELIZABETH BLACKWELL: PIONEERING PHYSICIAN, ABOLITIONIST, SUFFRAGIST

Elizabeth Blackwell was born in 1821 in Bristol, England, to Samuel and Hannah Blackwell. She was the third of nine children. Her father was a well-to-do sugar refiner, who could—and did—afford a good education to each of his children.

One night when she was eleven years old, a fire destroyed her father's business. In 1832, the family emigrated to the United States and set up a sugar refinery in New York City. Being devout Quakers, the Blackwell family believed that all men and women were equal in the eyes of God. True to their beliefs the family was anti-slavery.

In 1838 an opportunity was presented to Samuel Blackwell that allowed him to open a refinery in Ohio, where slaves would not be needed to harvest the sugar, so the Blackwells moved to Cincinnati. Three months later Samuel was dead of liver disease.

After her father died, in 1839, Blackwell took a teaching job in Kentucky to pay for medical school. She did not like the job. She moved in with a physician's family, using her time there to study from the family's medical library. She became active in the anti-slavery movement, as did her brother Henry Brown Blackwell, who married Lucy Stone, a suffragist, and the first woman from Massachusetts to earn a college degree. Lucy was the first recorded American woman to retain her own name after marriage. Another brother, Samuel Charles Blackwell, married another important figure in women's rights, Antoinette Brown, who became the first woman to become an ordained minister in the United States.

In 1845, Blackwell went to Asheville, North Carolina, where she read medicine in the home of Dr. John Dickson. Later she read medicine with John's brother, Dr. Samuel Henry Dickson in Charleston, South Carolina.

She attended Geneva College in New York. She was accepted there, because when the faculty put it to a student vote, and the students thought that her application was a hoax. She was subjected to rudeness and prejudice both from the faculty and the students. She is said to have replied that if an instructor was upset by student No. 156 wearing a bonnet, she would cheerfully remove her hat and sit at the back of the class but that she would not voluntarily absent herself from a lecture.

In January 1849, she became the first woman to earn a medical degree in the United States, graduating first in her class on January 23, 1849—two more "firsts."

Banned from practice in most hospitals, she was advised to go to Paris and train at La Maternite but had to continue her training as a student midwife and not as a physician. While she was there, she caught a serious eye infection from an infant she was treating, *purulent ophthalmia,* and she had to have her eye removed and replaced with a glass one, and her training was cut short.

In 1857, Blackwell, along with her sister, Emily, and Dr. Marie Zakrzewska, founded their own infirmary, the New York Infirmary for Indigent Women and Children. During the Civil War, Blackwell trained many women to be nurses and sent them to join the Union Army. After the war, Blackwell had time, in 1868, to establish a Women's Medical College at the Infirmary to train women doctors and physicians.

Also in 1857, Blackwell returned to England where she attended Bedford College, for a year in 1858, under a clause in the 1858 Medical Act that recognized doctors with foreign degrees practicing in Britain before 1858, she was able to become the first woman to have her name entered on the general medical council's medical register on January 1, 1859.

In 1869, she returned to Britain, leaving Emily in charge of the college. With Florence Nightingale, she opened the Women's Medical College. Blackwell taught at the London School of Medicine for Women and accepted a chair in Gynecology.

Elizabeth Blackwell retired in 1870 but still maintained her interest in the women's rights movement by writing lectures on the importance of education. She is also credited with opening the first training school for nurses in the United States in 1873. She also published books about diseases and proper hygiene. She was also pro-life.

In 1907 she was injured in a fall from which she never fully recovered and died in 1910. She is buried in St. Mun's churchyard on Holy Loch, Scotland.

EMMELINE PANKHURST: SUFFRAGETTE AND POLITICAL ACTIVIST

We are not here because we are law breakers; we are here in our efforts to become law makers.

Emmeline Pankhurst at her 1908 trial

...she shaped an idea for women of our time; she shook society into a new pattern from which there could be no going back.

Time, "100 Most Important People of the Twentieth Century"

Emmeline Goulden was born in Manchester, England, in 1858 on July 15. She was the eldest of five daughters and had five brothers.

She believed, however, that she was actually born a day earlier, which date coincided with the storming of the Bastille in Paris in 1789 by revolutionary women, which, she thought, would account for her own daunt-less spirit. Her mother's family, the Craine's, was from the Isle of Man and had been political activists for generations. The Isle of Man was the first country to give women the right to vote in national elections in 1881. Her father, Robert Goulden, was a merchant in Manchester, whose own family were also political activists. Goulden's mother worked with the Anti-Corn Law League, a pro-Free Trade organization, and Pankhurst's maternal grandfather was present at the Peterloo Massacre, where the British Cavalry charged the crowd protesting for Parliamentary reform. So we can see that Pankhurst came from an appropriate gene pool to carry out her "revolutionary" activities so zealously.

As part of the family's efforts to end slavery in the United States, they were visited by Henry Beecher Stowe. *Uncle Tom's Cabin* was regular bedtime reading for the Goulden children. Pankhurst herself was particularly inspired by Thomas Carlyle's *The French Revolution—a History*.

The Gouldens did not believe in giving the girls too much education, as they thought that girls were incapable of achieving the goals aspired to by boys. They believed that girls should learn about "making homes attractive." It seemed a rather odd mindset for such a politically active couple. Emmeline overheard her father saying to her mother that, "Such a pity that she wasn't born a lad."

When Pankhurst was fourteen, she came home from school one day just as her mother was going out to a meeting about women's voting rights at which the speaker was Lydia Becker, an early British suffragist. Emmeline insisted on attending. She later wrote, "I left the meeting a conscious and confirmed suffragist."

When Emmeline was twenty, she met Richard Pankhurst and they fell in love. Richard was a trial lawyer (barrister) who advocated women's rights, freedom of speech, and education reform. Richard was a confirmed bachelor in the sense that he felt that he could serve the public better if he was unmarried. Emmeline's mother criticized her for "throwing herself at Pankhurst" and suggested that she should cool the relationship down. Rather than get married, Emmeline suggested that they should enter into a "free union," but Richard said that such a relationship would exclude her from entering political life. The idea must have horrified her mother. So they married in 1879. Richard made two unsuccessful runs for parliament; the first was 1883 to represent Manchester, and the second in 1885 for Rotherhithe.

They had five children in ten years; Christabel in 1880, Estelle Sylvia in 1882, Francis Henry in 1884, and Adela in 1885. The Pankhursts decided that Emmeline was not to become a "household machine" and hired a domestic servant to free Emmeline up for her activities in the Women's Suffrage Society. Their son, Francis, died of diphtheria in 1888 caused by bad drainage. She gave birth to another son, in 1889, whom they named Henry Francis in honor of his deceased brother.

They lived with the Gouldens until Richard left the liberal party and argued a case against some wealthy businessmen in court. Robert Goulden was outraged, and the atmosphere became chilly. The Pankhursts moved to a small village and then to an affluent middle-class neighborhood in Russell Square, in London. The house became a meeting place for activists of all types. At this time, Emmeline decorated the house with fine oriental furniture and dressed the family in stylish clothing. Her daughter Sylvia later wrote that, "Beauty and appropriateness in her dress and household appointments seemed to her to be at all times to be an indispensable setting to public work." The Pankhursts hosted many notable people including US abolitionist William Lloyd Garrison, social activists Annie Besant and Henry Burrows, and French anarchist Louise Michel.

In 1888, the first national organization for women's rights, The National Society for Women's Suffrage, was split apart, as some of the membership felt that they should align themselves with political parties. Others argued that they should conduct themselves more moderately under "new rules." Lydia Becker stormed out of the meeting and formed a new group called the Great College Street Society, after the location of its headquarters, which would operate under the "old rules." Pankhurst aligned herself with the new rules group, now calling themselves the Parliament Street Society. But when it became apparent that the membership was not dedicated to suffrage for all women, not just the single ones, as they thought that married women had their husbands voting for them was sufficient, the Pankhursts formed yet another group, the Women's Franchise League.

The inaugural meeting of the WFL was held at their house in Russell Square and was addressed by William Garrison who warned that the abolitionist movement in the United States was being hampered by people who urged moderation and patience. Early members of the WFL included Josephine Butler, who concerned herself with the welfare of prostitutes and the repeal of the Contagious Diseases Act, and Harriot Stanton Blatch, daughter of American suffragist, Elizabeth Cady Stanton.

The WFL was labeled a radical organization, because it not only fought for universal suffrage but also rights for women in divorce and inheritance cases, trade unionism, and affiliation with socialist organizations. The more conservative group from the NSWS called them "the extreme left wing" of the organization. The Pankhursts riposted by calling the conservatives the "Spinster Suffrage Party," insisting that a wider assault on social inequities was required.

Financial considerations forced the Pankhursts to return to Manchester, where most of Richard's clients were located in northwest England anyway. Emmeline began to work with several political organizations and became well-known and respected in her own right as an activist. She briefly belonged to the Women's Liberal Federation (WLF) but found their policies too moderate and did not like the WLF's unwillingness to support Irish Home Rule.

She met and befriended Keir Hardie, a Scottish Socialist, who was the first independent Labour Member of Parliament to be elected to the Parliament of Great Britain. Hardie helped to create the Independent Labour Party. Pankhurst was very excited by the wide range of reforms that the ILF espoused, and she tried to join the party locally but was refused on account of gender. She did gain admission through the national party.

One of her first activities for the ILF was distributing food to poor men and women through the

Committee for the Relief of the Unemployed. In 1894, she got herself elected as a poor law guardian in the town of Chorlton-on-Medlock. She was appalled at the terrible conditions she found at the Manchester workhouse. She wrote:

> The first time I went into the place I (was horrified to see little girls of seven and eight years old on their knees scrubbing the cold stones of the long corridors…bronchitis was epidemic among them most of the time…I found that there were pregnant women in that workhouse scrubbing floors, and doing the hardest of work until almost their babies came into the world…Of course the babies are very badly protected…These unprotected mothers and their babies I am sure were potent factors in my education as a militant.

She immediately set to work to correct these awful conditions. Pankhurst established herself as a successful voice on the Board of Guardians.

After helping her husband with the second unsuccessful run for Parliament, she ran afoul of the law when she and two men violated a court order prohibiting ILP meetings at Boggart Hole Clough, a popular park in Blackley, Manchester. Richard represented the trio in court, and they refused to pay the fines. The two men spent a month in jail, but the judge, fearing backlash, was reluctant to imprison a popular and well-respected woman. She was asked if she was afraid of going to prison. She replied that it didn't frighten at all; in fact, it might prove to be an educational experience.

The Boggart Hole affair had taken a toll of Richard's health, and while Emmeline was in Switzerland with

Christabel visiting a friend, he took a turn for the worse and died as she was on her way home. Without her husband, Pankhurst felt the financial pinch, and she resigned from the Board of Guardians and took a job as registrar of births and deaths in Chorlton. She heard many tales of poverty and woe from the women reporting to her. She particularly noticed how the lives of men and women differed in cases of illegitimacy. In 1900 Pankhurst was elected to the Manchester school board and observed more discrepancy in opportunities between the genders. She knew that the right to vote for women must become law before all the inequalities could be rectified.

By 1903 she realized that all the years of moderate speeches by politicians did not produce any results—three bills for women's suffrage were defeated in Parliament. Pankhurst parted company with the ILP as the right to vote was very low on their agenda. The time for militant activism had arrived. She and some of her colleagues formed yet another group—the Women's Social and Political Union (WSPU). Deeds not Words became their permanent motto.

At first the militancy was non-violent and was limited to rallies, speeches, and protesting outside Parliament. Soon Pankhurst's three daughters became involved in WSPU activities, and things were ratcheted up a notch. Christabel was arrested for spitting in a policeman's face at a Liberal Party meeting. Adela and Sylvia were arrested during a protest outside Parliament. Emmeline was arrested while trying to force her way into the House of Commons in order to deliver a protest notice to the prime minister, H.H.

Asquith. She was charged with obstruction and sentenced to six weeks in prison. She found conditions in prison deplorable; "vermin, meager food, and civilized torture of solitary confinement and absolute silence" to which she and others were subjected. She realized that prison was an extra weapon in her arsenal as a means to publicize the urgency of women's suffrage. In 1908 she punched a police officer in the face twice to ensure that she would be arrested. During her trial she made her famous statement, quoted at the beginning of this chapter.

The WSPU actively protested against candidates for election in the ruling party and against any candidate who did not support woman's suffrage. They even managed to assist in the defeat of Winston Churchill in an election, his opponent remarking that Churchill's defeat was due, in part, to "those ladies that are sometimes laughed at."

In January 1908 Pankhurst and an associate, Nellie Martel, were attacked by an all-male group of Liberal supporters claiming that WSPU had cost them a by-election to a Conservative candidate. The women were beaten and had rotten eggs and snowballs stuffed with rocks thrown at them. In June of the same year, the WSPU increased its tactical intensity by breaking then windows at 10 Downing Street, the official residence of the prime minister. The perpetrators, Edith New and Mary Leigh, were sentenced to two months in jail. Pankhurst observed at their trial that male activists had done far worse things throughout British history.

In 1909 hunger strikes were added to the WSPU's repertoire, when Marion Dunlop was arrested for writing the Bill of Rights of 1689 on a wall of the House of Commons. As a protest to the dreadful conditions in the jail, she refused to eat. Fourteen women, imprisoned for smashing windows, immediately began fasting. Prison officials began force-feeding the women by tubes through the nose or mouth; the latter required steel gags to be inserted into the prisoners' mouths, a practice which was condemned by suffragists and medical professionals.

From1907 Pankhurst's life was filled with loneliness, sorrow, and illness, but she never gave up, and she never gave in. She sold her house in Manchester and lived out of as suitcase as she traveled round the country, staying in hotels, giving speeches, and participating in marches. She found joy in giving energy to others. As she planned a speaking tour of the United States, Harry became paralyzed from a spinal infection, but she had to go through with the tour to raise funds for Harry's treatments. The tour was a success, but Harry died on January 5, 1910, with his mother sitting at his bedside. Shortly after Harry's funeral, Pankhurst addressed a crowd of 5,000 in Manchester, and the Liberal Party hecklers who had come to disrupt her speech remained silent.

After the Liberal losses in 1910, left-wing journalist Henry Brailsford helped organize a Conciliatory Committee, which included 54 MPs from different parties, and they offered a Conciliation Bill in Parliament that seemed likely to pass. Pankhurst ordered all civil disobedience to be suspended pending the outcome of the legislation. When it failed, Pankhurst led three hundred protesters to Parliament Square where they were met with aggressive police resistance organized by the Home Secretary, Winston Churchill. The police punched the marchers, twisted arms, and pulled women's breasts. Pankhurst was allowed to enter Parliament, but Asquith refused to meet with her.

As successive conciliation bills were introduced, Pankhurst ordered cessation of militant tactics. When the second bill was in jeopardy, she instigated a fresh wave of window smashing, causing extensive property damage. The police raided WSPU's offices and arrested Pankhurst and Emmeline Pethwick-Lawrence, who were tried at the Old Bailey charges with conspiracy to commit property damage and were sentenced to serve time in Holloway Prison. Meanwhile, Christabel who was by now chief coordinator for the WSPU, fled to Paris and ran the operation from there. Inside Holloway, she staged her first hunger strike to improve conditions for suffragettes in adjacent cells. She was quickly joined by Pethwick-Lawrence and the other WSPU members incarcerated there.

In her autobiography she described the trauma caused by forced feeding; "Holloway became a place of horror and torment. Sickening scenes of violence took place almost every hour of the day, as the doctors went from cell to cell performing their hideous office." When prison officials attempted to enter her cell, she raised a clay jug over her head saying that, "if any of you dares so much as to take one step inside this cell, I shall defend myself."

Pankhurst was spared any further attempts to force-feed her. She continued to break the law and always fasted during her numerous incarcerations. The situation concerning the dozens of women on hunger strike in prison became so serious that Parliament enacted the "Cat and Mouse Act" (Prisoners' Temporary Discharge for Ill Health Act, 1913), under which suffragists were released from jail as soon as they became sick.

Now arson was introduced as a weapon of protest. In 1912, after Mr. Asquith had visited the Theatre Royal in Dublin, activists Mary Leigh, Lizzie Baker, Gladys Evans, and Mabel Capper attempted to blow the place up using a mixture of gunpowder and benzene. The device failed to explode, but the resultant fire caused extensive damage. During the same evening, Mary Leigh threw an ax at the carriage bearing the prime minister and the lord mayor, John Redmond.

During the next couple of years, a refreshment building in Regent's Park, an orchid house in Kew Gardens, a railway carriage, and several pillar boxes (mailboxes) were torched. There were many similar incidents round the country. Pankhurst and Christabel denied ordering these acts, but they were at pains to inform the public that they fully supported the arsonist suffragettes. A small ax inscribed with the words "Votes for Women" was placed into Asquith's carriage. The same slogan was burned into golf courses favored by MPs with acid. In 1914, Mary Richardson slashed the Rokeby Venus in the National Gallery as a protest to Pankhurst's imprisonment.

Some of the membership of the WSPU, including Emmeline Pethwick-Lawrence and her husband, disapproved of property destruction. When the Pethwick-Lawrences returned to England after a trip to Canada, they discovered that they had been expelled by Pankhurst, but to avoid a schism, they supported Pankhurst and the WSPU in public.

Then Adela left the organization for the same reason. Next came Sylvia, who spoke at a meeting of trade unionist and socialists in support of a labor organizer, Jim Larkin. Sylvia had been working with the East London Federation of Suffragettes (ELFS), which had close ties with trade unions and socialists. When she gave a speech on the same platform as Frederick Pethwick-Lawrence, Christabel became convinced, wrongly, that Sylvia was planning to form yet another group. Just released from prison, she was summoned to Paris where mother and sister were waiting for her. An acrimonious debate followed, which ended with Sylvia leaving the WSPU. Adela went to Australia and never saw her mother again. So the great family of activists was shattered.

When the First World War broke out, Pankhurst considered Germany the greater threat to freedom that the non-passage of a suffrage bill, so she ordered a cessation of civil disobedience and suggested that the ladies get behind the war effort and encourage young men to join the army. She also went to the United States in an effort to have the United States support the British and French against Germany. She also urged her American counterparts to suspend their agitation for suffrage. When the Russian Revolution brought the Bolsheviks into prominence and they showed signs of seeking peace with Germany, Pankhurst went to Russia to urge the Russian people to continue the fight and not accept terms from the Germans. That trip was sponsored by Prime Minister David Lloyd George.

"I came to Petrograd with a prayer from the English nation to the Russian nation, that you continue the war on which depends the face of civilization and freedom."

The press was divided with the left saying that Pankhurst was "tool of capitalism" and the right praising her devout patriotism.

On her return from Russia, she was heartened to learn that the 1918 Representation of the People Act was likely to become law. Under the Act, all men twenty-one years old on over got to vote if they had some minor property qualifications. Women over thirty years old got the vote, provided they were associated with someone on the electoral rolls. Full electoral equality would not occur until the passage of The Representation of the People (Equal Franchise) Act of 1928. The first woman elected to the House of Commons was Constance Makiewitz, representing the Sinn Fein party in Dublin, but she chose not take her seat at Westminster and entered the Irish Parliament, the Dail Eirerann. The first woman elected and to take her seat in the British Parliament was Nancy Astor, elected as a Coalition Conservative MP for Plymouth Sutton in 1919.

After the war, Pankhurst traveled promoting the British Empire and warning of the dangers of Bolshevism. When a bill passed allowing women to be elected to Parliament, many of Pankhurst's supporters urged her to run, but she insisted that Christabel run, and Pankhurst campaigned tirelessly for her. Christabel lost by a slim margin, and it sapped her energy.

She did make a run herself as Conservative candidate for Whitechapel—St. Georges, a district in east

London, but when Sylvia bore a child out of wedlock, claiming that the child was a triumph of eugenics, Pankhurst dropped out of the race.

Her health deteriorated, and she moved into a nursing home in Hampstead (northwest London). She requested the use of a stomach pump, which had helped her to feel better in prison. The nurses advised her against it, but Christabel felt duty bound to honor her wishes. Before the treatment could be administered, Emmeline fell into critical condition, and she died on June 14, 1928. She was sixty-nine years old. She was buried in Brompton Cemetery in London.

Her funeral was attended by hundreds of members of the WSLU and by both Christabel and Sylvia, carrying her baby. Adela did not attend. The *Daily Mail* described her funeral procession as a "dead general in the midst of a mourning army." The New York *Herald Tribune* called her "the most remarkable political and social agitator of the early part of the twentieth century and the supreme protagonist of the campaign for the electoral enfranchisement of women."

There is a statue of Emmeline Pankhurst in the Victoria Tower Gardens, which was unveiled in March 1930 by the prime minister, Stanley Baldwin, who said, "I say with no fear of contradiction that whatever view posterity may take, Mrs. Pankhurst has won herself a niche in the Temple of Fame which will last for all time."

ELIZABETH GARRET ANDERSON: PIONEERING PHYSICIAN, FEMINIST, MAYOR

Dr. Elizabeth Anderson was born Elizabeth Garret in 1836 in Whitechapel, London. Her father was a grain merchant and maltster of Aldeburgh, Suffolk, England. She was the first woman to gain a medical qualification in Britain and the first female mayor in England.

Anderson was educated at home and at the Academy for Daughters of Gentlemen at Blackheath. In 1859 Garrett heard a lecture by Elizabeth Blackwell on "Medicine as a Profession for Ladies." In 1860, after overcoming her father's objections and gaining his support, she decided to study medicine, an almost unheard of thing for a woman and considered on the edge of indecency. She entered medical training as a surgical nurse at Middlesex Hospital in London. She was the only woman in the class and was banned from full participation in the operating room. When she passed first in the exams, her fellow students had her banned from lectures.

She was refused admission at the Middlesex as a full student and many other medical schools to which she applied.

She studied anatomy, privately, at the London Hospital and with some of the professors at the University of St. Andrews and at the Edinburgh Extra-Mural school. She could not get a diploma to practice medicine, as the Royal Colleges of Physicians and Surgeons, and many other examining bodies, refused to admit her to their examinations. But the Society of Apothecaries allowed her to enter for the license of Apothecaries' Hall. She obtained her license in 1865, and this entitled her to her name entered on the medical register, the second woman, after Elizabeth Blackwell, MD, and the first woman qualified in Britain to do so. The Apothecaries promptly amended their rules so that no more women could be licensed.

In 1866 she was appointed general medical attendant to St. Mary's Dispensary. St. Mary's was a clinic to enable poor women to get help from qualified medical practitioners of their own sex, in that era a very unusual thing. The Dispensary developed into the New Hospital for Women, and Dr. Garret worked there for over twenty years.

She learned French, and in 1870 she earned her doctorate of medicine from the Sorbonne, in Paris, three months after Frances Hoggan, MD, obtained that qualification. In that same year, she was elected to the first London School Board, at the head of the poll for Marylebone, and was also made one of the visiting physicians of the East London Hospital for Children, but she found that both duties were incompatible, and she soon resigned them. She built a medical school for women in that year.

In 1871, she married George Skelton Anderson of the Orient Steamship Company co-owned by his uncle Arthur Anderson, but she did not give up her practice. She had three children, Louisa, Margaret, who died of meningitis, and Alan. Louisa also became a pioneering doctor of medicine and social campaigner.

In 1873 Elizabeth gained admission to the British Medical Association, which quickly voted to exclude any further female membership. Thus, Garrett was the only woman member for the next nineteen years. This was one of several instances where Garrett was able to enter a hitherto all-male medical institution, which subsequently moved formally to exclude any women who might to follow her.

Garrett worked steadily at the development of the New Hospital for women and at the creation of the London School of Medicine for Women, from 1874. Both institutions have since been handsomely refurbished, housed, and equipped. The New Hospital for Women, for many years, was staffed entirely by medical women.

In 1897 Dr. Garrett Anderson was elected president of the East Anglian branch of the British Medical Association.

On November 9, 1908, she was elected mayor of Aldeburgh, the first female mayor in England.

The movement for the admission of women to the medical profession, of which Dr. Garrett Anderson was the indefatigable pioneer in England, extended in her lifetime to all of North America and Europe, except for Spain and Turkey.

She died in 1917 and is buried in Aldeburgh.

MARIE CURIE: NOBEL LAUREATE EXTRAORDINAIRE

The most inspirational woman in science

New Scientist Magazine, 2009

…She was probably the only person who was not corrupted by the fame that she had won.

Albert Einstein

A Family Affair

Marie was born Maria Sklodowska in Warsaw in November, 1867, the fifth and youngest child of Bronislawa and Wladylaw Sklodowski. Both parents were teachers; her father taught mathematics and physics, and her mother operated a boarding school for girls in Warsaw. Her parents lost their property and fortunes through various Polish national uprisings, condemning Maria and her siblings to a difficult struggle to get ahead in life.

Marie made a deal with her sister, Bronislawa. She would give her sister financial support during her medical studies in Paris in return for reciprocal assistance when Bronislawa graduated. Marie took a series of jobs as a governess to well-to-do families. During her internship with the Zorawskis, a landed family related to her father, she fell in love with their son, Kazimierz, and he with her. His parents would not countenance such a thing, as she was virtually penniless. They dismissed Sklodowska.

At the beginning of 1890, Bronislawa, now married, invited Marie to come and live them in Paris. Marie declined, as she would not be able to afford the fees for university tuition. She tutored and studied at the "Floating" University, an underground educational enterprise, the purpose of which was to educate Polish youth in subjects which might clash with the ideology of the ruling establishments. Marie also began her practical scientific training at the Museum of Industry and Agriculture in Warsaw.

When Marie received a "Dear John" letter from Kazimierz Zorawski, who she had been hoping to marry, she decided to go to Paris after all. She stayed with her sister briefly before renting a garret and proceeding with her studies of physics, chemistry, and mathematics at the Sorbonne (the University of Paris).

Zorawski went on to earn a doctorate in mathematics and became rector of Krakow University and president of the Warsaw Society of Learning. He never got over Maria, and as an old man, he would sit before her statue in front of the Radium Institute, now the Maria Sklodowska-Curie Institute of Oncology, which Maria had founded in 1932, headed by her physician sister, Bronislawa.

Marie studied during the day and tutored in the evenings. In 1893 she was awarded a degree in physics and went to work in an industrial laboratory. Continuing her studies at the Sorbonne, she earned a degree in mathematics in 1894.

In that same year, she met Pierre Curie, who was an instructor at the School of Physics and Chemistry in Paris. Sklodowska had been investigating the magnetic properties of various steels, and Pierre himself was very interested in magnetism, and as a result, they became attracted to each other, as it were. Marie thought, incorrectly, that if she returned to Poland, she would be able to enter Krakow University and work in her chosen field of study. She was denied entry, solely because she was a woman. The trip did have a significant benefit though, as their absence made their hearts grow fonder, and they married in July 1895. There were two hobbies they both enjoyed, long bicycle rides and foreign travel, but Marie had found love and a scientific partner, on whom she could utterly depend. Bike rides and travel notwithstanding, the new couple rarely left their lab.

In 1897 Sklodowska-Curie gave birth to a daughter, Irene, and in 1904, another daughter, Eve. Irene Joliot-Curie won a Nobel Prize for Chemistry in 1935 and was a professor at the Faculty of Science until her death in 1956.

Eve Curie became a journalist and was the only family member that did not pursue a career in science. She wrote a biography of her mother. During a visit to the United States in 1921 with her mother and sister, Eve captivated every one of the male persuasion and was dubbed "the girl with the radium eyes."

Marie Sklodowska-Curie now focused her research on the radioactive properties of uranium. In 1898, the Curies announced the discovery of two new elements, polonium, named in honor of her native Poland, and radium, which they named for its intense *radioactivity*, a term which they coined. They had no idea of the ill-effects on their bodies that working so closely with radioactive elements was to have.

In 1903, Marie was awarded her doctorate of science from the Sorbonne, and Pierre, Marie, and Henri Becquerel, who discovered that uranium salts emitted X-ray like emanations, were awarded the Nobel Prize in Physics. She was the first woman to be awarded a Nobel Prize. The Curies shared their financial proceeds with needy acquaintances, including students.

The Curies worked assiduously to separate one tenth of a gram of radium chloride from a ton of ore. By 1910, working alone, as Pierre had met with a fatal accident in 1906, she had isolated pure radium metal. Generously, she did not patent her process so that the scientific community could do research unhampered.

The Sorbonne gave Pierre a professorship and his own laboratory, in which Marie became director of research. After his death in 1906, the Sorbonne physics department decided to retain the chair created for him and pass it to Marie, with full control over the laboratory, and thus another first for Sklodowska-Curie—the first woman professor at the university.

In 1911, Sklodowska-Curie was awarded the Nobel Prize in Chemistry, thus becoming the first person to win or share two Nobel Prizes, and she is one of the only two people to be awarded a Nobel Prize in two different fields (the other being Linus Pauling, for Chemistry and Peace). The French Academy of Sciences held fast to its prejudice against women, and Marie failed by two votes to be elected a member. Ironically, it would be a doctoral student of Marie's, Marguerite Perey, who would become the first woman member of the academy in 1962.

In 1910 Sklodowska-Curie had an affair with a married physicist, Paul Langevin. It lasted for about a year. Langevin was a former student of Pierre Curie. Once the press got wind of it, it developed into a major scandal and was exploited by her academic opponents. She was five years older than Paul, and she was characterized as a home wrecker, and possibly even Jewish. Much later, Marie's granddaughter, Helene Joliot, herself a nuclear scientist, married Langevin's grandson, Michael Langevin, also a nuclear physicist.

During the First World War, "the war to end all wars," Marie pressured the French government for the use of mobile radiography units to treat wounded soldiers. The units were powered by radon. Sklodowska-Curie carried unprotected tubes of radon in her pockets, and she commented on the "pretty blue-green light that the substances gave off in the dark."

Maria Sklodowska-Curie died in 1934 of aplastic anemia—a condition certainly related to her exposure to radioactivity.

Her work has had a profound effect on science, as well as on the way in which society regards women. To achieve her many attainments, she had to break down a multitude of barriers placed in her way, solely because of her gender both in France and Poland.

Awards and Honors:

> Nobel Prize in Physics (1903)
> Davy Medal (1903)
> Matteucchi Medal (1903)
> Elliot Cresson Medal (1903)
> Nobel Prize in Chemistry (1911)
> French Legion of Honor
> Honorary Doctorates at;
> Lwow Polytechnic (1912)
> Poznan University (1922)
> Jagiellonian University, Krakow (1924)
> Warsaw Polytechnic (1926}

And, of course, the homage of all of us.

CONDOLEEZZA RICE: THE LIVING LEGEND

*Let your light so shine before men that they may see
your good works and glorify your Father in heaven.*

Jesus Christ

*Talent hits a target no one else can hit; Genius hits a
target no one else can see.*

Arthur Schopenhauer

This is the story of an incredibly gifted woman. Her light is like a beacon on a hill, and it is there for all of us to see. The term genius is a rather pale description of her mental capabilities, and to find a person with similar attributes, we would have to go back in history about two thousand years. Looking for a role model? Look no further.

In her current ministry, she gives of her knowledge, experience, and love everywhere she goes. She is a rare and exotic wild bird that must always fly free. She can achieve anything that she puts her mind to. She is not content to excel at whatever she does but always strives to be the best that there is.

Condoleezza Rice is a warm and loving person but with a mind like a steel trap and is as tough as old shoe leather when she needs to be. Like all great leaders, she knows exactly how to handle most situations. Mary Beth Brown, in her excellent biography, *Condi,* coins the term "steel magnolia" which is a perfect two-word description of Dr. Rice.

If the reader wants to read a partial biography of Condoleezza Rice, I would recommend Mary Brown's book, which is written with warmth and obvious affection, but remember that are some more chapters yet to be written—hopefully a lot more.

It has been said and written that Rice comes from humble origins. I am not at all sure that that is the case. If being born to two extremely loving, well-educated, and successful people, who were also the very best parents a child could possibly wish for is a humble beginning—then she was. Condoleezza's name in derived from an Italian musical direction, *con dolcecezza* , which directs the musician to play "with sweetness."

Rice has written a book about her parents, John and Angelena Rice. So far be it for me to write about them, except to say that Angelena was a beautiful woman and a true queen, and that John was a prince among men. Condoleezza Rice was a very lucky little girl indeed to have them. They protected her from the racial ugliness and brutality prevalent in the South in the early sixties—no "whites only/colored only" experiences for their little girl. But they were at pains to make sure that Condi was well aware of the situation in which thugs like Bull Connor held sway. Of course, his and the actions of other ignorant perpetrators of violent bigotry actually did a lot to advance the civil rights movement, because it aroused the anger of a nation and got the attention of the White House.

Speaking of the White House, there is a quotation of Condi's that I want you to hold in your mind, even if it is the only thing that you remember from this book. She said:

"My parents had me absolutely convinced that, well, you may not be able to have a hamburger at Woolworth's, but you can be president of the United States."

Angelena wanted Condi to attend the local segregated elementary school, but the principal thought that at four and a half, she was too young. Angelena took a year's leave of absence from her teaching job and tutored her daughter at home. Education was a passion for both John and Angelena, and they have passed that on to their daughter.

In May 2006, Dr. Rice gave the commencement address at Boston College, and stressing the importance of education, she laid out her "five important responsibilities of educated people:

> Find your passion and follow it. Do something that you love.
>
> Use your reason. We have been taught how to think and not what to think. .
>
> Cultivate humility and reject false pride.
>
> Be optimistic and avoid cynicism. Look ahead with bright hope.
>
> Serve others. It is our responsibility to close the gaps of justice and opportunity that still divide our country and our world.

Condi's homeschool schedule was rigorous: schoolwork in the morning, lunch, schoolwork in the afternoon—no playtime. She learned to read quickly using a speed-reading machine. She had already started learning the piano, thanks to her grandmother, Mattie Ray's influence, at three and a half.

Condi loved learning and absorbed knowledge like a sponge. Her self-discipline was ironclad, and her focus intense. From an early age, she was exposed to culture, having lessons in ballet, tap dancing, French, flute, violin, and ice skating. Condi never sloughed off, studying all day and practicing piano into the evening. Her young friends often had to wait an hour or two before Condoleezza was ready to come out and play. Most importantly, Angelena taught her daughter deportment, manners, and respect for others—in fact, to be a lady.

John Wesley Rice III was a doctor of divinity and a football coach. He and his daughter were in a mutual adoration society. He taught her everything that there is to know about football and encouraged frank discussions of religion and particularly the life and role of the historical Jesus. John was always available to neighborhood youths to encourage them to better themselves.

John and Angelena traveled every summer to the University of Denver in order to pursue their goal of obtaining master's degrees in education. Meanwhile, Condi was taking ice skating lessons and practicing three hours a day. John obtained his master's degree in 1969 and a job as assistant director of admissions at the University of Denver. The Rice family moved out West.

Condi was enrolled at St. Mary's Academy, a Catholic school with high academic standards. She was a straight-A student, with self-confidence, poise, and polish, an accomplished pianist, skilled ice-skater, and a good tennis player. She won a piano competition, the prize for which was to perform a piece with the Denver Symphony Orchestra.

John and Angelena wanted Condi to graduate early and start college, but she wanted to graduate with the rest of her class and accordingly embarked on a really tough self-imposed schedule; ice-skating in the early morning, then over to the University of Denver for two part-time classes. In the afternoon she went to St. Mary's for high school classes, followed by piano practice in the evening.

At this time, Condi wanted to go to the Julliard, but John was against the idea, believing that she could be more successful in some other endeavor, despite the fact that he had just bought her a Steinway grand piano for $13,000.

At fifteen she enrolled full-time at the University of Denver, with piano being her major at the Lamont School of Music. During one class, the professor expounded on physicist William Shockley's view that blacks were inferior to whites intellectually, a view with which he evidently agreed. This was too much for Condi, who stood and eloquently informed the professor that he should not make such statements without proof and evidence. In fact, she went on to explain to him that she was the one who could speak French and could play Bach and was better at his culture than he was and that these things could be taught regardless of race. The professor had no answer to that.

At the end of her sophomore year, she participated in the Aspen Music Festival. There she encountered young musical prodigies, and she faced up to the fact that although she was a very good, she was not Carnegie Hall material and began casting around for another major to spark her interest.

At the beginning of her junior year, there came into her life "a tide which taken at the flood," and she began a course in international politics with Josef Korbel, the noted Sovietologist. When Korbel gave a lecture on Josef Stalin's rise to power, Condi was hooked. She would continue to play the piano for pleasure, but her course in life was clear. At nineteen she graduated from college with BA in political science—Phi Beta Kappa; she won the Political Science Honors Award; and membership in Mortar Board.

Condi went to the University of Notre Dame, a college which had been thoroughly researched by John and Angelena. The school had an excellent Soviet Studies department, the faculty of which included political philosopher Gebhart Niemeyer and political scientist George Brinkley. In 1975 she earned her master's degree in political science.

In the summers of 1977 and 1978, during her doctoral work, Condi was an intern first for the State Department and then for the Rand Corporation. In 1981, at the age of 26, she received her PhD in political science from the Josef Korbel School of International Studies at the University of Denver. The title of her doctoral dissertation was "The Politics of Client Command: The Case of Czechoslovakia 1948–1975."

She had become an expert on the Soviet Union, the Soviet Military, and weaponry in general. She even learned to speak Russian.

She applied for an assistant professorship at both Stanford and Harvard. The latter did not respond, but Stanford snapped her up in a heartbeat. Some people are adept at missing boats, Harvard.

Condi started teaching political science and loving it. Academe is her passion. Among her mostly liberal colleagues, she became known as "Condi the Hawk" because of her conservative views on foreign policy. She was promoted to associate professor in 1987 and to full professor in 1993.

In 1985, she attended a meeting of arms control experts at Stanford and captured the attention of Brent Scowcroft when she disagreed with him on something he had said. Scowcroft quickly discovered that Condi was not only brilliant but an expert on weaponry and Soviet affairs.

Brent Scowcroft had been national security advisor to Gerald Ford, and with the election of George H. W. Bush, he returned to the White House once again in the same post. He asked Dr. Rice to be his Soviet expert on the US National Security Council. President Bush was very taken with by Condi and relied heavily on her during his dealings with Mikhail Gorbachev and Boris Yeltsin.

During the period of the fall of the Berlin Wall and the collapse of the Soviet Union, Rice served as director and then as senior director of Soviet and Eastern

European affairs of the National Security Council in George H. W. Bush's administration and as a special assistant to the president on National Security Affairs. She was the key aide to secretary of state, James Baker's, policy in favor of German re-unification. The president introduced Dr, Rice to Gorbachev as "the one who tells me everything I know about the Soviet Union."

Because of considerations of tenure at Stanford, which made absences of more than two years a disqualification, Rice returned to Stanford in 1991. She was taken under the wing of George Schultz, who was Ronald Reagan's secretary of state (1982–1989). Schultz was a fellow of the Hoover Institution, a think tank founded by Herbert Hoover, and he included her at the luncheons held every few weeks attended by intellectuals to discuss foreign affairs.

Schultz, a board member of Chevron, recommended her for a seat on the board. Chevron was negotiating a $10 billion development deal with Kazakhstan. Rice knew the president of Kazakhstan through her travels to Russia, went to Kazakhstan, and secured the deal. Chevron named a super-tanker in recognition of her services the *Condoleezza Rice*. Condi was also appointed to the boards of Transamerica and Hewlett-Packard.

At Stanford in 1992, Rice was on a search committee to find a replacement for the outgoing president, David Kennedy. The committee finally recommended Gerhart Casper, the provost of the University of Chicago. Casper was so impressed with Dr. Rice that he asked her to become provost of Stanford. When she assumed that role, the college was $20 million in the red, and Rice said that she would balance the budget in two years. Many people scoffed at the notion. Condi made many tough decisions, and not a few people unhappy, but at the end of two years, Stanford had a $14.5 million surplus.

During George W. Bush's presidential campaign, Condi took a one-year's leave of absence from Stanford to be his foreign policy adviser. The group of advisers that she led was called The Vulcans, in honor of a statue of Vulcan that overlooks her home town—Birmingham, Alabama.

At the Republican National Convention, Rice gave a speech which included the assertion that, "American armed forces are not a global police force, they are not the world's 911."

On December 17, 2000, Dr. Condoleezza Rice was appointed national security advisor. She quickly earned the soubriquet "Warrior Princess," which reflected her strong nerve and regal demeanor.

Understanding that al-Qaeda posed a serious threat to the security of the United States, Rice met with President Clinton's National Security Council counter-terrorism coordinator, Richard Clarke to discuss the issue. She decided to keep Clarke on as the chief counter-terrorism point man in the Bush administration. She also retained his entire staff.

Her job as NSA was to act as mediator between the different cabinet members and advisors who comprised the National Security Council (NSC): Vice President Dick Cheney, Secretary of State Colin Powell, Secretary of the Treasury Paul O'Neill, Secretary of Defense Donald Rumsfeld, Chairman of the Joint Chiefs of

Staff General Richard Meyers, CIA Director George Tenet, and other senior officials.

She gathered information from these men, condensed it into a concise report, and presented it to the president, in order for him to make a decision on the matter. It was not her job to present her own opinion but to be able to recognize the various opinions within the administration. The president trusted Condi so much that he had her become a public representative on security matters.

Because of her gentility and soft manner of speech, there were some who sought to undermine her authority. There is a story that one treasury official foolishly took her on. With a smile on her face she sliced him and diced him, with sweetness, of course—the Steel Magnolia.

During the summer of 2001, there was a lot of intelligence indicating that a big terrorist attack on the United States was forthcoming. Yet as she remarked, the terrorist chatter was frustratingly vague. Nevertheless, federal agencies and departments were put on a high state of alert. The Defense Department warned the military, at least five times, that al-Qaeda was planning an attack. The CIA was directed to aggressively increase its covert operations against al-Qaeda.

On September 11, 2001, Rice was scheduled to address the School of Advanced International Studies at John's Hopkins University on the topic of missile defense. She was also planning to warn of attacks by car bombs, suitcase bombs, and gas attacks similar to the Sarin attack in Tokyo. The address never took place, but on April 29, 2002, she finally mounted that podium and said, among other things, that democracies tend to get complacent, forgetful, and lazy, quoting George Washington: "Democratic people must *feel* before they will see." On September 11, America felt and America saw.

On January 25, 2005, Dr. Rice was approved by the US Senate, eighty-five to thirteen, to become the sixty-sixth United States secretary of state. Her first six months was spent meeting with NATO leaders in Brussels, conferring with European Union officials in Luxembourg She made stops in Paris, Rome, Jerusalem, and London where she met with Tony Blair at 10 Downing Street.

She traveled extensively, spreading the gospel of democracy and transformational diplomacy, which she defined as, " working with our many partners round the world, and building and sustaining democratic, well-governed states that will respond to the needs of their people and conducts themselves responsibly in the international system."

Her diplomacy was based on strong presidential support and is considered to be a continuation of the style of Henry Kissinger and James Baker.

Condoleezza Rice has appeared four times on "Time 100," *Time* magazine's list of the world's most influential people, one of only nine people to do so.

She is now back at Stanford doing the thing she loves the most—teaching.

BIBLIOGRAPHY

Brenton, Lancelot C. L., *The Septuagint with Apocrypha*, Samuel Bagster & Sons, Ltd., 1851

Brown, Mary Beth, *Condi*, Thomas Nelson, Inc., 2007

Churchill, W. S., *A History of the English Speaking Peoples*, Dorset Press, 1956

Mulford, Prentice, *Thought Forces*, G. Bell & Sons, Ltd., 1934

The Holy Bible, New King James Version, Thomas Nelson, Inc.1979

Winwar, Frances, *The Saint and the Devil*, Harper and Brothers, 1948